Prologue

On a cold, blustery day in January 1961, John F. Kennedy stands on a platform in Washington, D.C., and is sworn in as the new President of the United States.

Here I am, a sixth grader, sitting in class watching it on television. Most kids are bored, doodling in notebooks, passing notes, shooting spitballs. And then there's me, or I, or whatever. I am, as my older brother would say, transfixed by the image of a dapper President on TV.

Let the word go forth from this time and place, to friend and foe alike, that the torch has passed to a new generation of Americans—born in this country, tempered by war, disciplined by a cold and bitter peace, proud of our ancient heritage and unwilling to witness or permit the slow undoing of those human rights to which this nation has always been committed. . . .

I know Kennedy is talking about his generation, the people like my Dad who fought in World War II, but he might as well be talking to me, to us, telling us that there's a new battle to be fought, in the streets and schools and workplaces of our own towns and cities, and that the human rights belong to us.

> Let both sides explore what problems unite us instead of belaboring those problems which divide us . . . Let both sides unite to heed in all corners of the earth the command of Isaiah —to 'undo the heavy . . . burdens and let the oppressed go free.'

This is John F. Kennedy as bright as the noonday sun, and his speech hits me like a ray. I know the words will stay with me for the rest of my life.

I want to "undo the heavy burdens and let the oppressed go free," and someday I know that I will have my chance.

Chapter 1

Baseball in St. Louis on a hot August Saturday afternoon is, as my Grandpa Will likes to say, as close to playing in the Devil's yard as you can get. But this is Mama Ev's kind of baseball game. A late-summer nail-biter, even though if I had dared bite, she would've slapped my hand and said, "Clayton Banks, you'd chew those nails down to the quick if I wasn't here to stop you!"

Anyway, it's nail-biting time, but I'm behind home plate trying to figure out why Lo-Tone is shaking off my signals. See, Lo-Tone and I go way back. Well, I should say Anthony Lee Coleman and I go way back, as far as the first grade at Carwell Grammar School. It's not like we finish each other's sentences or anything. But each knows what the other is thinking. Like when we play basketball and I can flip him a pass without looking because I know he will be there.

Lo-Tone got his nickname from the boys back in the third grade because of his low—and I mean low—voice, in the St. Paul's African Methodist Episcopal Children's Choir.

So, here we are, on this hot August day in 1963, a month before our first day of high school. I keep throwing down one finger—fastball—and he's just shaking his head. If we beat this team—Calvary Baptist—we're on to the championship game of the Church League. And here's Lo-Tone dismissing my expert calling of the game. I mean, Mr. Carter, our coach, lets me call the game, so you'd think that Lo-Tone would trust my judgment. Pitchers! They think they're so smart.

"Time!" I yell.

The umpire yells, "Time!"

I take off my mask as I trot out to the mound. Lo-Tone eyes me all the way in.

"Clay, this guy can turn on my fastball. Why you throwin' down the fastball, Poindexter?" Lo-Tone asks me.

Lo-Tone is the only person in the world who could call me Poindexter and get away with it. Not even John-Two, my older brother, can get away with that. Lo-Tone calls me that when he thinks that I'm thinking too much.

"Lo-Tone, this guy is anxious," I start. "We're up by one run. They've got two outs and nobody on base. The whole thing is on his shoulders, and he's scared. He's expecting you to throw a curve because he knows you know that he's a fastball hitter. He hit your curve foul. He's expecting another. So let's give 'em the gas!'"

Before Lo-Tone can utter another word, the ump screams out, "Fellas, ya'll havin' a prayer meeting? Let's play ball."

"Lo-Tone, trust me," I say, and give him a wink. He holds his glove out and I drop the ball in his mitt. We're ready to roll.

Everret "Big Ham" Hammond, Jr., stands outside the batter's box and takes some practice swings as I squat behind the plate.

"Oh, you think plannin' with Anthony is going to get me out?" he says. "Ya'll got another think coming! You saw how far I took that weak curve for a ride."

"Shut up, Ham," I say, pounding my fist in my glove. "You hit it foul anyway."

"Both you boys hush up and play ball," says the ump, Reverend Jenkins. He points at the pitcher and signals him to play ball.

I don't even put down a finger. I pound my glove and set up on the inside of the plate. Lo-Tone winds up and lets fly with a fastball.

The ball moves toward the inside and Ham is fooled. He shifts his weight farther to the right and takes an off-balance swing. The ball hits my mitt and makes that sweet pop.

"Strike two!" the ump yells.

I stand up and throw the ball back to Lo-Tone. "That away, Lo-Tone."

I look at Ham and he's glaring at me and trembling. He's lost his senses, and he's right where I want him. Ham is a great hitter . . . until you rattle him.

I get down in my stance. I look at Lo-Tone and flash two fingers—a curve. Lo-Tone looks at me with a straight face. He's not giving anything away because he knows Ham is looking at him as well.

Lo-Tone is good at hiding his pitches, which is one of the reasons he's a good pitcher. You don't pick up on what he's going to do until the ball's on the way. Guys with bad eyes—the ones who can't pick up the ball quickly—they're dead meat. Ham, on the other hand, is the kind of guy that you have to fool. Both pitcher and catcher. Two cats versus one big dog.

Lo-Tone winds up. I start to set up on the inside, but then I move to the outside and set my glove. Lo-Tone fires, and it's a beauty.

Ham is surprised again; I can tell because he's moving and shifting. This time he's moving to meet the ball, and he just catches up and manages to pop the ball straight up in the air.

Ham's quick reflexes fool me. I really didn't think he'd catch up to the ball, and I hate pop-ups. It's the weakest part of my game. Funny thing, though. Whenever I get nervous, I hear Mom.

Watch the ball all the way into your mitt, she'd say as we'd practice in the backyard when I was a little kid.

I look up immediately and follow the ball back behind the plate. I block everything else out. It's just like being in the back yard.

Don't take your eye off the ball. Don't be scared. That's it. You got it.

"Out!" Reverend Jenkins says.

I run out to the mound with the rest of my teammates to greet Lo-Tone and congratulate the team on making it to the championship. Everybody pats us on the back. I hand the ball to Lo-Tone and say the words we always say when we win a game together.

"Brilliant performance, Mr. Coleman," I say with a bad British accent.

"A well-called game, Mr. Banks," he says with the same bad accent.

We laugh. I toss him the ball. Then, the last thing I do no matter what the score is to look up in the sky.

"Good game, Mom," I whisper and wink.

"Good game, Clay. Good game, Lo-Tone."

Ah, it's the sweet voice of Della Amanda Tillborn. Oh, brother, she is—as Romeo says about Juliet—the sun, with those long, curly locks, and skin, smooth as silk and the color of mahogany . . .

"I said, 'Good game, Clayton,' " she says, slowly and loudly. I'm always dazed around Della. I almost always stutter around her.

"Clayton would talk, except he's so choked up about the win and all," Lo-Tone says, with his arm around my shoulders. "He's so weak that I have to prop him up."

"Get off," I laugh. Then I look at Della. "Ah, thanks."

Della smiles. I smile. Della smiles some more. I smile some more. I have nothing to say. Well, I have a bunch of mushy stuff to say that I'm not going to say—ever. So I smile—like an idiot.

"Hey, I know how fun this must be, standing around and lookin' foolish, but I'm thirsty," Lo-Tone says, breaking the silence. "Ya'll wanna go down to Jake's Place and get a soda?"

I'm still looking at Della. She turns her eyes to Lo-Tone.

"I'm up for that. What about you, Clay?" she says.

"Uh . . . uh."

I feel like such a clown.

"Sure, he wants to go," Lo-Tone says, putting me between himself and Della. "The winning pitcher on one side, and a very pretty young woman on the other, how could a fella turn us down?"

Della smiles, and my ears heat up.

"Uh, yeah," is about all I can muster.

I've been like this around Della since we were in third grade. She and her family moved up here from Nashville. Her father, Dr. Earl Tillborn (Dad says not a real doctor, but a Ph.D), is a professor at Monroe Teachers College downtown. He's also the school's assistant basketball coach and a pretty cool dude. I sometimes go over to Della's house to shoot hoops with him and Della's older brother, Earl Jr.—E.J.—but really I just kinda try to case my sight on Della.

Which is what I'm doing as the three of us groove down the sidewalk to Jake's Place. Jake's is *the* hangout. There are other places to go to get a soda, but those places don't have a Jake Taplin.

Chapter 2

The bell on the screen door tinkles as we walk in. Jake appears from the back room, the ever-present green dish towel around his neck and the toothpick clamped between his lips. "Well if it isn't Josh Gibson and Satchel Paige, and—oh, my goodness—is that the beautiful Lena Horne with you two?"

That's Jake. The smooth South Carolina gentleman, quick with the compliment, and the maker of the finest cheeseburger-and-greasy-fries combo in the known universe. But the cool thing about Jake is that he knows everybody and he treats everybody like they were family.

Jake loves baseball. In fact, he used to play with and against Josh Gibson and Satchel Paige in the old Negro baseball leagues. He was a catcher for the Homestead Grays, the Chicago American Giants, and the St. Louis

Stars. He's given me a lot of pointers on controlling the game, like studying batters and opposing pitchers. Jake says the game is both physical and mental. Jake always tells me: You can swing the biggest stick in the world, but if you're not there mentally, then you're going to get beat.

"Hey, Jake, we won! It's on to the championships for us!" I say as the three of us sit at the counter. Lo-Tone starts spinning the red stool next to him.

"Boy, do you know how many times I have told you not to do that!" Jake says. "Do your parents let you spin their chairs?"

Lo-Tone has been doing that as far back as I can remember.

"Sorry, Jake. We don't have stools like this. I keep asking my parents to get some, but they don't listen to me."

"Chile, and right they shouldn't," Jake laughs. "Now, what'll it be? Or are you all just content soaking up my air?"

"Three sodas is about all we can afford," I say.

"All right, young squires and lady. Grape Nehi for Clayton, and for you two?" Jake asks Lo-Tone and Della.

"Coke," says Della.

"That sounds good," says Lo-Tone.

"Two Cokes and a Nehi coming up," says Jake. "And I'll throw in a plate of fries because you won."

"Thank you, Jake," Della says, and smiles.

Jake bows elegantly. "Della, you know how to make a

tired old coot feel young."

Della just looks down and smiles. I can tell she is charmed.

Jake pulls the sodas from the fountain and sets them on the counter. We all take deep sips.

"So, Clay, you looking forward to starting high school?" Della asks.

"I guess so," I say flatly.

"You guess so? I can't wait."

"Uh. Well, I'm a bit nervous."

"I'm not!" Lo-Tone blurts out.

"That's good, Lo-Tone," Della says, but she turns her attention back to me. I'd rather not say anything. I'd rather she ask Lo-Tone why he's not afraid of high school.

"So, Clay, why are you nervous?" she asks.

"I don't know. Maybe because I want to be somebody."

"Of course you do," Della says. "I want to be somebody too. In fact, I have it all planned out." Her eyes flash as she says this. I notice the gold flecks around the edges and the way they're tilted, like a cat's. I can't think of anything to say—she's too pretty. But it's OK because she keeps talking.

"For my freshman and sophomore year, I'm going out for the pom-pom squad. I figure that will get me the experience I need. Then in my junior year, I'm going to make the cheerleading squad."

Lo-Tone and I just look at her.

To understand why Della's words have left Lo-Tone and me speechless, you'll have to understand something about our community and our time. We live in Wilson Park, the Negro section of Middlefield, which is a suburb of St. Louis. The word "section" is sort of misleading, because there isn't a law that says we have to live here and only here. But, to be honest, we aren't really wanted anywhere else in Middlefield. In fact, even though we live in Middlefield, we're called Wilsoners, while only the whites go by the name Middlefielders.

Anyway, the Wilsoners and the Middlefielders have a strange relationship. Both places have their right side and wrong side of the tracks. Both places have doctors, barbers, banks, and stores, though we do shop in downtown Middlefield.

And we live separate school lives until high school. That's the most interesting thing. There's only one school in Wilson Park, and it only goes through eighth grade. The Middlefield school district didn't think there were enough Negroes, or blacks, as we are called now, to create a separate high school for them and, until fairly recently, they wouldn't allow them into Middlefield High. So for the longest time, blacks from Middlefield had to take a 25-mile trolley ride into St. Louis to attend Sumner High School. Can you imagine having to commute an hour and a half each way just to go to school? It didn't leave much time for homework, let alone having fun. But that's the way it was for blacks, and there wasn't much you could do about it.

It was a combination of tradition and law that kept the races apart, separate but equal, as they said, which refers to the 1896 Supreme Court decision *Plessy* v. *Ferguson.* I wrote a school paper about it in seventh grade. The justices ruled against Homer Plessy, a black man who had been fined 25 dollars for sitting in a train car that was reserved for whites. The court said that laws requiring separate facilities for blacks did not violate the Constitution as long as the facilities were equal. This ruling became known as the "separate but equal" doctrine. The result was that separate public washrooms for blacks, separate drinking fountains, separate entrances to public buildings, and separate schools were all guaranteed by the law of the land. Blacks and whites couldn't eat together, watch a movie together, ride in a train together, or learn together.

In 1954, the Supreme Court landed the first blows to help end this kind of craziness. That was the year the court struck down the "separate but equal" doctrine with the case of *Brown* v. *the Board of Education of Topeka.*

Led by Chief Justice Earl Warren, the court ruled in favor of Linda Brown, a young girl who wanted the right to attend a school near her home rather than the blacks-only school that the Topeka, Kansas, Board of Education forced her to go to.

Well, two years after that, in 1956, the Middlefield school district, in fear of a similar lawsuit, decided to let blacks go to Middlefield High.

Grandpa Will was a lawyer then. It was a few years

before he retired. The folklore is that Grandpa Will met with the school board and defiantly told them that he was going to whip 'em all in court if they didn't open the high school to Negro students. They shivered and caved in.

Here's what really happened: Grandpa delivered one of the great speeches about the U.S. Constitution, freedom, and common sense and decency ever written. Also, it's probably the longest speech ever written. How do I know? He gives this speech every year at Thanksgiving.

Halfway through the meeting, the board caved in, not because Grandpa Will was right but because they feared a lawsuit. Of course, in our family we joke that Grandpa's speechifying left the board members so tired and hungry that they just wanted to go home.

There was grumbling in Middlefield at first, until later that school year when a black basketball player, Raymond Mitchell, scored 25 points and grabbed 18 rebounds to lead Middlefield to its first conference title in 30 years.

So the school was integrated. But how integrated? Many of the best football and basketball players over the past couple of years have been blacks, but at the games— where both whites and blacks play on the same field and march in a unified band—Wilsoners and Middlefielders don't sit next to one another in the stands. They yell at the same time. They moan at the same time. But they don't share a seating section.

15

Sure, everyone's happy when a black scores big
points, but no one of my color ever has captained the
team. No black ever has been made drum major, or class
president, vice-president, or treasurer. Just last year, a
black girl was named to the student council, but she got
in by just one vote. And Middlefield High School has
never had a cheerleader darker than alabaster. Lo-Tone
and I know, as everybody knows, that there are plenty of
people in the school who want to make sure that
integration fever won't spread to cheerleading.

"Whoa," Lo-Tone says softly. "Not even Carla
Griffins could make the squad."

Carla's story had spread like a hot wind through
Wilson Park when it happened a few years before. Carla,
Lo-Tone's next-door neighbor, was one of the best-
looking girls in her junior class and the best pom-pom
girl, black or white. She could leap higher, kick wider,
and do more back flips in a row than any other girl in
the history of the school. Everybody liked her, and both
black kids and white kids thought of her as their friend.
But when she tried out for the cheerleading squad, it was
like she had stepped over a line. They couldn't keep a
black girl from trying out; there was no rule against it.
But she was the first to dare it.

In the days leading up to the tryouts, no one talked
of anything else. The tryouts had always been public in
the past, big events that people looked forward to like
any sports competition. But the cheerleading coach
shocked the school by announcing that this year they

16

would be closed. No one would be allowed to watch. Needless to say, Carla didn't make it. When the lucky girls' names were announced, the judges said the winners had scored highest on grace, stamina, gymnastic ability, and team spirit. But one girl—a white girl—who had tried out and not made it told everyone that Carla clearly had been the best of all. People stopped talking to the girl. They said her comments were just sour grapes, and they accused her of trying to make trouble because she hadn't made the squad.

As for Carla, she took her defeat with her usual grace and was as nice as ever. But she had had the bad luck or bad sense to overstep her place and make the white folks look bad. It was as though she had held up a mirror to the white community, and the people who didn't like what they saw blamed her. Carla suddenly wasn't so popular any more, either.

"Things are changing. My mama and daddy both say so," says Della.

For some reason, even though my palms are sweaty and my mouth is dry, on this subject I find words to speak. "Not fast enough," I say. "John-Two says we all gotta do our part."

"That's what I mean," Della says.

"I don't mean by doing silly high-school stuff like becoming captain of the basketball team or getting onto the cheerleading squad. I want to be someone special, not a jock, but someone people look up to, like Martin Luther King."

"Whatever, Professor. You figure you'll be the next Reverend King by your junior year?" Lo-Tone asks.

Della giggles. Oh, man, it's a sound like music, like a meadowlark's song. But why can't *I* get her to laugh like that? Instead, she's laughing *at* me, and I get annoyed.

I say, "Do you guys remember sitting in class back in sixth grade and watching Kennedy's inauguration? It's been two years, but I've never forgotten it. He talked about a new generation creating a better future and stuff. I want to be one of the people who changes things, not somebody who goes along with somebody else's game."

Jake brings over the fries. His hand's not even off the plate before I grab the ketchup bottle and squeeze. Ketchup spurts out of the bottle with a noise like a long, wet, snotty sneeze, and the fries are buried in red.

Della smirks behind her hand and Lo-Tone laughs out loud. "Hey, Professor!" he says. "Ever think of asking if the lady likes ketchup?"

"Oh, unh . . . I . . . "

"That's OK," Della says sweetly. "I really need to get going anyway." She gets up and smoothes her dress. I stand up but I can hardly look at her. I'm looking at the big, messy pile of fries smothered in ketchup, and I feel like a huge idiot.

"I'll see you around," I say to the fries. Della sweeps out the door, and I watch her, awash in sunlight, pass by the window.

"Oohh whee! Now that was smooth, my friend," Lo-Tone laughs. He picks up the ketchup bottle. "Mind if I use that technique next time I want to get rid of a girl?"

I grab the bottle from his hand and slam it on the table. "I wasn't thinking."

"That's a new one for you, Poindexter. Doesn't matter anyway, right? Because if you liked her, I'm afraid you had already blown it with the 'silly high-school stuff' remark."

I can't tell if Lo-Tone is making fun of me or not. I've always tried to keep my feelings for Della a secret, but it's hard to imagine Lo-Tone not knowing. It's better to steer clear of that topic, so I continue: "But it's true. How can we change the world when all we're thinking about is sports and cheerleading?"

"I'd hate to hear what Coach Carter would have to say about that," says Lo-Tone.

"You know what I mean," I say. "I keep going back to what President Kennedy said: 'Undo the heavy burdens and let the oppressed go free.' And I think about Dr. King leading the marches and the protests down South, and I want to be a part of that, but I don't know what to say, much less do."

"You're talking crazy," Lo-Tone says. "Maybe things aren't perfect, Clay, but how do you know they'll get better and not worse with all these changes you're talking about?"

"I just don't believe this is the way it should be," I say.

"But is it so bad? Clay, we've got it good. We live in nice houses, wear nice clothes, and we've got a little change in our pockets. We've got it made, Clay. Stop trying to invite trouble."

19

Lo-Tone would get an "amen" from my Dad on that point. It's not that Dad doesn't care. He just doesn't want to see all that blacks have built be taken away. He seems to think that in time things will change. But let's face it. This life is wrong now if you can't do what you want to do, or live the way you want to live. I'm lucky, but there are a whole lot of blacks in Wilson Park, and elsewhere, who don't have it as easy as I do.

Chapter 3

For some reason, I'm dreaming about giant trout. Massive, multicolored trout with big mouths.

I know how strange that sounds, but lately I've had this recurring dream where I am swimming in Lake Winnebago with Lo-Tone and Bobby Petway, another good friend of mine. They are standing along the dock and I'm way out. Way, way out. And I keep trying to wave to them, but these giant trout keep blocking my view. There are no trout in Lake Winnebago. I don't like to eat fish. I don't even like to go fishing with Dad and Grandpa Will. I just sit in the boat and read. So I'm not very happy being surrounded by trout. Now pancakes are in my way. Umm, pancakes. Big fluffy, golden pancakes.

Hey, who's tickling my feet?

"John-Two!"

"How's it going, little brother?"

. It's so great to have John-Two back from Fisk, if only for a month. He's the coolest big brother in the world. Sure, he can be a pain-in-the-behind from time to time, like when he uses big words and makes me look them up in the dictionary—just like Dad does. Or when he thumps me on the ear in church because he knows that if I yelp I'm going to get it.

But John-Two is the most. Like when he taught me how to swim when we were kids, out at Lake Winnebago. If it wasn't for him, I never would have figured out my eight times table. He helped me bury my turtle, Pokey. He helped me through Mom's death.

That happened on March 12, 1962.

I remember coming home from choir with Lo-Tone. I don't remember it being warm or cold, if I was wearing a coat or sweater or what color shirt, if I had on cords or jeans. I do remember Grandpa Will and Mama Ev, Mom's parents, waiting for me on the porch. Mama Ev was crying, and Grandpa Will was trying not to cry.

I knew it was something wrong with Mom. I don't know why I didn't think of Dad. They would've cried just as much, but for some reason I thought *Mom.* Apparently, something had ruptured in her brain. She had fainted, stopped breathing, and died. Dad had found her in the living room.

The funeral was open-casket, and there must've been 100 people crammed in St. Paul's A.M.E. The service was really nice, with people getting up and saying all sorts of wonderful things about Mom.

The burial was, well, a burial. I closed my eyes mostly and tried to think of other things. That's how Mom taught me to handle difficult things, like shots at the doctor.

Close your eyes and think of something nice.

During the prayers, I thought of her pancakes: fluffy, golden, good.

"What are you thinking about?" John-Two whispered.

"Pancakes," I whispered. "You know, Mom's pancakes."

Everybody came back to the house to eat. The women of the church had cooked a feast: ham, fried chicken, a roast, macaroni and cheese, potato salad, greens, lima beans, elevendy-billion types of pies. And I couldn't eat a thing. I just sort of kept quiet. I wanted to be left alone, and I bristled whenever people told me how I should feel.

"Oh, son, it's God's will that she was taken from us."

I would nod my head. *Shut up. Please stop talking to me. Go away!*

Lo-Tone ran interference for me, getting people out of the way. I'm sorry, it may sound ungracious and ungrateful, but I didn't want to be bothered, and Lo-Tone broke me free by setting picks.

"Mrs. Jones, have you had the peach cobbler? It's delicious, why don't you go try some?" Or, "Clay, I think your Dad needs you in the other room."

And, you know what? He was the only person

outside my family who didn't ask me how I felt, or worse, told me that he understood how I felt. Lo-Tone had lost his grandmother a year earlier. It was tough for him, but I think there is something different about losing your mom.

Despite Lo-Tone's best efforts, people did manage to talk to me. And the thing that made me blow my cool the most were the people who kept telling me how great Mom looked in her casket. After hearing it one too many times, I snapped at somebody. I don't remember who. I just snapped.

"Tell me something?" I asked in a low growl. "Do you really think she looked good, or do you all have nothing else better to say?"

People turned and looked in horror. I remember the expression in Dad's eyes when I said it. He wanted to tear up, but he couldn't because he had to be strong. He was the father. John-Two and I were the sons. We were allowed to be withdrawn. But Dad had to be strong, to shake hands and not let anyone know that he was all torn up inside.

"You all heard me. How is it that she looked good?" I screamed. "She's dead. She couldn't look good. She's dead!"

Dad grabbed me by the shoulder and pulled me close to his face. "Now you stop. Stop now."

Our eyes met and locked. The world around us stopped.

"Did she look good to you, Dad?" I said with my teeth clenched.

That was the only time I've ever been disrespectful toward my father. John-Two was the hard-headed one who argued. I was not a rebel. I never gave Mom or Dad a lick of trouble. But there I was, there we were.

I'd never seen Dad that mad at me. But I knew he agreed with me. The dead, no matter how beautifully they are made up, are still dead. The woman in the casket wasn't the mom who taught me how to catch a pop fly, read, sing, and know the difference between a soup spoon and dessert spoon.

That woman wasn't the wife who laughed at Dad's jokes no matter how awful, who stole kisses from him when she thought we kids weren't looking, and who calmed him down when the world got cross with him.

They had seen only a made-up face, not the mom we loved.

"Dad, let me take him outside," John-Two said.

That was the first time I noticed him being there. This was our moment: Dad and me.

Dad's grip loosened, and I bolted out of the house and tore down Harrison Avenue. I'd never run that fast. I'd never cried that hard.

I think I ran a mile before I stopped, gasping for air, my brain racing with a thousand thoughts, not the least of which was that Dad was going to kill me for making him look like a fool in front of all those people. And I was very hungry. But at least I was all cried out.

"Dang, little brother, you've gotten faster."

John-Two huffed and puffed and blew.

"Hey," I said weakly.

"You all right?"

"Mom's dead. You're away in Nashville. Dad's going to kill me. Other than that, my life's fine. How 'bout you?"

I blurted all that out while still trying to catch my breath, and it only made me gasp harder.

We both panted and gasped and gasped and then we both started to catch our breath, but John-Two hadn't answered my question.

"John-Two, I'm scared," I said in my normal voice.

"Oh, Dad's not going to . . . "

"I'm not talking about Dad. I'm scared that I'll forget Mom."

"No you won't. You're being irrational."

"There you go with the big two-dollar words. How's this? You're being irritating."

"Come on, Clayton. Do you really think you'll forget Mom? All she did for you, for us? The time she spent caring for the two of us and Dad? Those memories aren't going anywhere."

I didn't say anything. I just soaked up what he had to say.

"For me, all those squares sitting around looking at Mom, but not thinking of Mom. I couldn't take it. You know, I didn't look in the casket? I didn't. I didn't want my last memory to be of that. That's not how she was. I looked at the choir and thought about Mom singing. Was that bad?"

"Nah, little brother, that's you. We all grieve in different ways. I listened to some Ella Fitzgerald last night and thought about Mom reading."

We both sat on the curb on the sidewalk and looked up. It was dusk. The birds were flying to their nests. A few cars passed us.

"Everything will get better, right?" I asked.

"Yeah, little brother, we'll be all right. Let's go home."

"You think Dad's gonna kill me?"

"Soon as everybody leaves. Then I think your time is up, Jackson," he laughed. "Nah, it's OK. Dad understands more than you think."

He was right. Most people had already left by the time we got home. I told Dad I was sorry. He nodded, smiled a little, winked, and said we'd talk about it later. We never did.

Chapter 4

Hey, hey, Mama Ev!" I yell, running into the kitchen.

Grandpa Will is making pancakes, and Mama Ev is sitting at the breakfast table reading the *Post-Dispatch*. John-Two and I run down the steps. I'm in my gym shorts and a St. Louis Cardinals warm-up shirt, the kind the players wear underneath their jerseys. This is the best way to eat breakfast.

"Hey, hey, yourself, child," she says and pecks me on the cheek.

"I see you've found the catch of the day," she says and winks at John-Two.

"Who's up for pancakes, eggs, and bacon on this fine Sunday morning?" Grandpa asks, twirling the batter-coated spatula in his hands.

He needn't have asked. He is constantly accusing John-

Two and me of being the hungriest children in the world. Since Mom died, Grandpa Will and Mama Ev have made it a Sunday tradition to come over to our house before we all walk down to St. Paul's. Later we eat Sunday dinner over at their house, which is only a couple of blocks away.

We also eat together on Tuesdays, at our house. On Mondays and Thursdays, Mrs. Bates, who lives next door, cooks dinner for her husband and us. On Wednesdays and Fridays, Dad comes home from the office early, and we cook together, usually something pretty easy like hamburgers or pork chops with potatoes or succotash.

John-Two reaches into the pantry and takes down five plates. I get five juice glasses and five glasses for milk. Then I get the juice and milk out of the refrigerator.

Grandpa Will fixes everybody's plate except for Dad's.

"Hey, where's Dad?" I ask, directing the question to no one in particular.

"He had an emergency tooth extraction this morning," Mama Ev says. "He should be back any minute."

"Should we wait?"

Everybody looks at me with that are-you-out-of-your-tiny-little-mind look.

"Sorry. Dumb question."

We all sit around the dining room table. Without saying a word, we all hold hands and Grandpa says grace.

"Dear gracious Lord: Smile upon us and feed our souls. For the nourishment of our bodies. Christ our Lord, we thank thee."

We all say together: "Amen."

"Dig in!" I yell, and I start shoveling food into my mouth. John-Two is not that far behind.

"You boys act . . . " Mama Ev starts to say, but John-Two and I cut her off and finish the sentence, "Like we were raised by wolves!"

"No, they act like they were raised by bears."

That voice is Dad's, or as the rest of the town knows him, Dr. John Franklin Banks, Sr., the only dentist in Wilson Park.

"And you're the biggest bear of them all, I take it," John-Two says, getting up from the table to hug Dad.

It's a good sight to see. John-Two hasn't been home since Easter break. Right after school let out, he joined a bunch of other kids from Fisk University and Tennessee State down in Alabama to work for a student civil-rights group called SNCC—which you say, *snick.* SNCC stands for the Student Nonviolent Coordinating Committee. It's a group that was formed in 1960 to work for equal rights using nonviolent means.

Dad says John-Two doesn't need to get involved in other people's business, but it's his call to make. And I know Dad's been worried, despite the fact that John-Two calls or writes once a week. His letters have been full of stories of voter registration drives, marches, and protests.

Dad grabs a plate, hurries to the kitchen, and comes back with a plateful of food.

"How'd it go this morning?" Mama Ev asks Dad.

"I'll spare you the gory details, but I had to pull two of Mr. Johnson's teeth. If he'd have followed any sort of hygiene over the years, he wouldn't be in so much pain. I mean, he's forty-two. I'm forty-two." He shakes his head. "Well, those people."

Ah, the first argument is about to begin. It's a set-up from Dad. It has to be.

"Those people?" John-Two says between bites. We've all learned over the years how to hold a debate and eat at the same time. "How are they different, Dad? Oh, they don't have as much money as we do, so we're better, right?"

Grandpa Will, Mama Ev, and I turn to Dad to see the next move.

"So, how's the summer been? Learn anything?"

Change the subject? That was a strange move. But, OK, let's see how John-Two responds.

"It's been a wild ride, Dad. We've been sprayed by hoses. Had dogs turned on us. Been spit on and threatened. I was even punched by some white kid at a lunch counter in Montgomery."

At this Mama Ev gasps. "Thugs," she says, shaking her head.

"Did you hit him back?" I ask, punching at the air.

"No."

What? I say to myself. *If it would've been me, I would've kicked that guy's butt.*

John-Two says, "I think SNCC is right—'By appealing to conscience and standing on the moral nature of human existence, nonviolence nurtures the atmosphere in which reconciliation and justice become actual possibilities.' " He loves to impress us all by quoting from SNCC's statement of purpose. "Dr. Martin Luther King believes in nonviolent protest. Gandhi practiced it in India and won his country back from the British. We cannot become what our oppressors are. If we do what they do—beat people, kill people—then our movement falls apart. We are no better than the people we are fighting against."

"So, what does that make me?" Dad asks. "I flew with the Red Tails during World War II. We fought against the Nazis. Both your grandfathers fought during World War I. Are we as bad as the people we fought against?"

"Ah, Dad, you know that's not what I mean. That was different. That was a declared war."

"So, you'd change your tune if there were another Civil War? If Kennedy declared a war against the South, and sent the army down there the way Eisenhower did in Little Rock, except they start shooting, then it's OK?"

Dad was referring to the time back in 1957 when President Dwight D. "Ike" Eisenhower, whom Kennedy succeeded in office, sent troops to Little Rock, Arkansas, to integrate a public high school. Grandpa Will was there in Little Rock, part of the team of lawyers who helped the process.

As Grandpa Will tells it, the school board in that city had admitted nine black students to its Central High School. Everyone thought it was going to be quiet, but people went absolutely nuts.

The Arkansas governor, Orval E. Faubus (you should hear the way Grandpa Will spits out the name as though it was the Devil's himself), brought in the national guard to surround the school. The governor said it was done to protect the kids from angry mobs. But the guard also kept out the black students. So Ike placed the Arkansas National Guardsmen under federal control and sent down the army's 101st Airborne Division to help keep the peace.

I was just a tyke, but I remember Mom and Dad and everybody else thinking that there was going to be a civil war.

John-Two continues, "Now you're twisting my words, Dad. I said that we didn't want to become like the people who oppress us. If we throw sticks and bricks back, then they'll start shooting. And in the end, nothing will get done. We work for our rights . . . "

"And what rights do you not have? You go to one of the best schools in this country. You've got good clothes, a nice home when you need it, and you've never been hungry."

"You see what I mean," John-Two says, looking at the rest of us like he was pleading his case to the Supreme Court. "The black folks down South . . . "

"Oh, here you go with the 'black' thing," Dad shoots back. "We're Negroes. You got a problem with that word?"

"We were called colored for the longest time," Mama Ev steps in. "Did you like that? Let the boy finish his point."

"Thank you," John-Two says. He's shaking because he wants Dad to understand where he's coming from. John-Two takes a deep breath and slowly begins to make his case.

"Dad, we're down there helping folks who don't have much. I appreciate everything you've given me. But if I don't do something when I see people in need, then what good am I? Look, I know that Mr. Johnson didn't have enough money to pay full price for his dental work. That's the reason you've got a sliding scale—to help people like him. Am I right?"

Dad sits stone-faced. He's not going to budge. He's the Sphinx. John-Two doesn't let up, and I'm interested to see where he's going.

"Well, my point is that you're reaching out to people who need your help. Isn't that what you taught us? To reach out?"

Dad's still sitting stone-faced. Then he looks at his watch.

"You boys get a move on, clean the dishes, and get dressed for church. Will, thanks for breakfast this morning. We'll pick you all up on the way to church."

That's it. Case closed. Everybody except Dad moves from the dining room to the kitchen, plates and glasses in hand. I grab Dad's plate.

"John-Two," Dad says.

John-Two turns.

"I'm glad you're home, son."

John-Two smiles, thumps me on the ear, and throws me the drying towel.

"Come on Jackson, let's get to steppin'."

To understand the relationship between John-Two and

Dad, you have to understand where each one is coming from. There is a lot of love and respect between them, but they disagree on so many things.

Dad was born in 1920 in Clayton, Alabama. He was the only son of Papa Marvin, a farmer, and Mama Sallie, a much better farmer. They owned a very small plot of land, where they raised some chickens and a milk cow and grew some crops.

Papa Marvin and Mama Sallie also had six daughters. Later Papa Marvin and Mama Sallie moved to Detroit to live with my Aunt Erma, who is the oldest child, born two years before Dad. Papa Marvin and Mama Sallie both died before I was old enough to know them.

Dad and his sisters were lucky enough to graduate from high school. Apparently, this was pretty unheard of, since a lot of kids back then worked from the age of about 14 on to keep their families afloat.

College, however, was a whole different matter. There wasn't any money for Dad and his sisters to go to school. The University of Alabama; Tuskegee Institute, a black college in Alabama; and Hayes Teachers College in Nashville all had scholarships available. Dad was qualified academically to go to all three, but as it turned out, he didn't have a choice of which college he would go to.

Remember, Dad, the rest of his generation, and those who came before—blacks and whites—lived with the doctrine of "separate but equal." It's not as though the court created the separation between blacks and whites. After all, blacks were enslaved until the Thirteenth

Amendment freed them after the Civil War. But even then, freedom didn't mean that blacks were able to do what they wanted.

"Separate but equal" was not the brightest of ideas, because those who didn't want blacks to get ahead provided only the bare minimum of "equal." No matter how much we protested, they'd point to the Supreme Court ruling.

Grandpa Will calls the doctrine "separate but unequal" and fought as a lawyer with the NAACP—the National Association for the Advancement of Colored People—to change the laws that were based on it. But they weren't changing much in the 1940s. The University of Alabama, along with other universities in the South, did not admit black students. So Dad had a choice between Hayes and Tuskegee. Or so he thought.

Way back when—but it's not like the attitude has gone away—some blacks set themselves apart based on—get this—how dark or light their skin was. Or how straight or curly, soft or coarse, or loose or tight their hair was. Dad had straight hair that curled at the end, but he couldn't pass the brown-bag test. Dad is the color of a Hershey chocolate bar (and Mom said he was twice as sweet), and that meant he was darker than a brown paper bag, which meant that he wasn't going to go to Hayes. It's not like they put a bag next to his skin and said, "Too dark, you're out!" No, they just eyed him up and said, "Well, we just don't have enough openings in the incoming freshman class. Maybe you should look at Tuskegee."

Think about this: Dad, no matter how smart he was, wasn't allowed into the University of Alabama because he was black. Then he was told, in a roundabout way, that he was not allowed into Hayes because he was too poor and too dark of a black.

Dad did so well at Tuskegee that he graduated with a degree in biology in three years. He started college at 17 and graduated at 20. Man, was that cat too smart!

Anyway, he earned his way to McNichol Medical College, in Nashville, to study dentistry, which is—and here's another one of my brother's favorite words—ironic because McNichol is located just across the street from Hayes.

The year is 1941, and Dad is running from the Hayes library to an afternoon class at McNichol. He bumps into a beautiful young woman named Eleanor Marie Maxwell or, as I would later call her, Mom. To make a long story short, he falls in love. She thinks he's a big goof. He falls more in love. They meet at a school dance. She tries to brush him off but can't resist his charms. She agrees to one jitterbug. Then she agrees to another. And another. Then a slow dance. A year later, they're married.

And a year after that, Dad's back at Tuskegee training to be a fighter pilot, and Mom is living with Grandpa Will and Mama Ev in Wilson Park taking care of John Banks, Jr., or as we call him, John-Two.

Dad doesn't talk about World War II too much. He's proud that he served with the 99th Pursuit Squadron in Italy and in England, escorting bombers to their targets deep into Germany. Dad is credited with shooting down two German fighters by himself and got half credit for shooting down another. In fact, his squadron never lost a bomber to an enemy fighter. That was quite a feat, considering that the army air corps didn't think that blacks had the mental capacity to fly, much less participate in dogfights.

And you'd think that the United States, as a nation, would be grateful. But just like his father and Grandpa Will, both of whom had fought in World War I, Dad and the other black veterans came home to a nation that still, in many places, didn't allow him to sit, eat, or sleep where he wanted. The St. Louis area is a crossroads of East and West, but also of North and South. While it didn't seem as bad for Dad and Mom and John-Two back then, it was segregated and there was another world that we could not enter.

Dad went back to McNichol to finish his last year of dental school. Then he came back to work in Wilson Park, and I was born five years later. Dad's been very successful so far, and he doesn't see a need to live with or work with white people.

So for Dad, the separation of the races is no big deal. He's into Booker T. Washington, the founder of Tuskegee, who said, in the same year as the court ruled on *Plessy*, that blacks and whites could be as separate as the fingers on the hand. In fact, we'd all be better off if we all lived peaceful and separate lives, or so goes the argument that Dad and a lot of other people make.

John-Two and his friends at Fisk and other colleges, blacks and whites, are taking a whole different approach. They're down South signing up poor people to vote, organizing protests, and marching for basic civil rights. John-Two wrote me a letter telling me how a guy he knows, a white friend of his from Boston, was beaten and killed by some racist thugs. They put a sign around his neck with the word *traitor*. Two more people he knew, young blacks from Detroit, were found shot to death in a car. Even John-Two wrote that he'd been in a "scrape or two" with the Ku Klux Klan, the violent secret racist organization.

It's no wonder that a great many Wilsoners and Middlefielders go through their lives not caring about much outside their own lives. For one thing, they're scared of what happens to black people who take a stand. For another, they wonder, What's the use? "Things won't get better, so why rock the boat?" is a prevailing sentiment.

Well, I care. The report that I wrote on *Plessy* v. *Ferguson,* for example, got an A from my teacher. But the principal of the school thought I should've picked a more appropriate subject to write about. He didn't think that "stirring up the past" was a good thing. But it was a history class!

I think what I'm looking for is my moment to stand up and make a statement about what I believe in. But I have to wonder why I don't stand up myself?

Dad's typical response to the issue of desegregation and integration is, "I don't have anything against the whites, but they have their ways, and we have ours." He doesn't think that Martin Luther King, Jr., is wrong. "He's just misguided," he says.

For Dad, things won't change because he believes that people basically want to live apart. "The lion doesn't lay down next to the tiger! Big cats need to live separate lives."

"But Dad," John-Two would say when debating Dad at the dinner table, "Tigers and lions aren't even located on the same continent!"

"My point exactly!"

I would just look confused.

I didn't then, and I don't now, know what to believe. Dad has good points about the way things are. But John-Two makes an excellent case for the way things could be. And that's where I am looking. No disrespect to Dad, but I know things can be different, better somehow.

As much as I love John-Two, he can be—and here's another one of his big, fancy words—strident. He's always been that way, ever since I've known him. He's always believed that the world shouldn't be the way it is. He was the one who would protect other kids from the class bullies. He'd take on two or three big guys at once, and he'd even whoop them. And man, could he play football. Both sides of the ball too: fullback on offense, bruising linebacker on defense. I once saw him catch a little pitch five yards behind the line of scrimmage, sweep right, then turn back and sweep left, stiff-arm three guys, and run 50 yards for a touchdown. Then he kicked the extra point and made a bone-crushing tackle on the kickoff.

And he's the kind of guy who took the game seriously, until the whistle blew. Then he'd be the first guy to shake your hand and tell you, "good game."

People would say, "You were so brave out there," and John-Two would shrug it off and say that football isn't about bravery. Gandhi was brave. Frederick Douglass, who started an antislavery newspaper back before the Civil War, and Harriet Tubman, who led hundreds of slaves to freedom along the underground railroad, were brave. Rosa Parks was brave to refuse to give up her seat to a white man on that Montgomery, Alabama, bus in 1955. John-Two would say that football is just a game, and that he wouldn't take it so seriously that he couldn't walk off the field thinking about something else, like poetry.

That didn't make him the favorite of the coach, who thought he'd grow up to be one of those beatniks up in New York, bangin' on a bongo all day and saying, "Hey, daddy-o."

Well, John-Two does read a lot—the beatniks, but also Richard Wright, Countee Cullen, and the other black writers of the Harlem Renaissance. He listens to cool jazz, the blues, and even that square stuff from the Metropolitan Opera on the radio.

"Little brother, education is the key," he says when I tease him about doing egghead things. "The more you know, the better. It's a big world, Clayton. Experience it."

My brother, my dad, and I are all book smart, but there's that something, that unexplainable something, inside of us that makes us tick.

John-Two is the rebel, the St. John the Baptist, the Joan of Arc, the guy who is way out front of the battle. Sometimes too far out in front, unwilling to listen to reason, but with a strong heart.

Mom once said that I was the healer and philosopher. I'm always trying to soothe people's nerves and always thinking and analyzing; sometimes overthinking, Lo-Tone says.

Dad is the straight-arrow, hard worker. We all have elements of one another inside us. Both Dad and John-Two are set in the character department, but I still feel like I haven't defined who I'm supposed to be. Instead of this big goofy kid who floats through life and *thinks* about changing the world, I want to be someone who actually *participates* in changing the world, like Grandpa Will and Mama Ev. She taught mathematics and history at Sumner High School and walked in protests with her husband. And Dad fought in World War II against the Nazis. Mom was a member of the NAACP, and she, too, marched and organized and wrote letters. John-Two spent the summer in the heart of all that craziness.

And then there's me. I'm ready to do anything. But what?

Chapter 5

And now the women's choir will sing the hymn 'Onward Christian Soldiers,' " Reverend Johnson says. Thank goodness this is a sit-down song, because it gives me time to daydream . . . and sneak peaks at Della Tillborn.

Lo-Tone and I are ushers this Sunday, which means we pass out the collection plate and help the elderly people to their seats and to the communion rail. It also means we get to sit in back, away from the prying eyes of our parents. It's not like we can get away with too much, though. I just sit and doodle and look at Della. Lo-Tone goes through his baseball "exercises." Little annoying exercises, like trying to see how much his peripheral vision stretches and gripping a baseball to work the tendons in his wrist and fingers.

"That was lovely, ladies," Reverend Johnson says

when the song was finished. "The church appreciates your talents on this fine Sunday morning. Mrs. Carter will now read the announcements."

I like Mrs. Carter a lot. She's much older than Mom, more Mama Ev's age. Besides being the wife of our baseball coach, she was one of the people who helped me out after Mom died. She really listened and didn't tell me it was wrong to be mad at God. Then she slowly helped me realize that God didn't take Mom away from me.

"It's fate, child," she said. "Pure and simple. You don't know what's going to happen. If you did, life wouldn't be worth living. Your job now is to grow up to be the man that your mother wanted you to be."

Mrs. Carter has a powerful voice that moves through you like thunder sometimes, but like a summer breeze on other occasions. I guess it comes from being a speech teacher at Sumner High School for 25 years.

Mrs. Carter steps up to the podium and opens a blue folder. "Good morning, St. Paul," says the summer breeze, "and isn't this a beautiful day the Lord has made for us? Let us rejoice and be glad."

Most of the people in the church agree by saying, "Amen."

"I have just three announcements this morning. First, the Women's Missionary Society will hold its annual bake sale next Sunday, before church, beginning at nine-thirty A.M. There will be pastries of all types and sizes available. So bring your appetites and your change and help support the Women's Missionary Society.

"Second, I am pleased to announce that the boys' eighth- and ninth-grade baseball team defeated Calvary Baptist, three to two, last night. Bobby Petway drove in the winning runs with a clutch hit in the sixth inning. The battery of Clayton Banks and Anthony Coleman kept Calvary at bay. Our young men will face St. Mark's Catholic Church next Saturday at three P.M. at Kennilworth Park for the Church League Championship. Congratulations and good luck. You boys stand up. Brothers and sisters, let's give them all a round of applause."

We all stand up, and everybody cheers us on. I feel sort of sheepish, almost embarrassed. John-Two, Dad, Mama Ev, and Grandpa Will cheer loudly. As I turn and wave at the rest of the church, I catch Della looking directly at me. I think I'm going to faint. I look away, and then look back, and she's still checking me out.

"If you can make it to the game, come cheer the boys on," Mrs. Carter says.

"Now, the final announcement: St. Paul's and a few other local churches plan on sending buses to Washington, D.C., to participate in the March on Washington for Jobs and Freedom on the twenty-eighth of August. I can't tell you how important this day is going to be, for the nation and for the black people. Prominent leaders, including the Reverend Doctor Martin Luther King, Junior, will deliver major speeches. This day promises to go down in history as a turning point in our country. Will you be one of those who heed

45

the call? The cost to attend this event with the church is twenty dollars. You need to have your reservation in by Sunday, August eighteenth." Mrs. Carter closes her blue folder and smiles. "These are the announcements for this week."

You know how you sometimes hear something or see something and you instantly think, *This is it!*? Grandpa Will says that that feeling tells you you're experiencing a defining moment in your life, a moment that tests and builds your character at the same time. I think . . . no, I *know* this is what I want to do. Mrs. Carter said it best when she asked if we were going to heed the call to the march. I've heard the call. I want to go.

Now, how I'll get Dad's permission to go is a whole 'nother problem.

After church, Dad, Grandpa Will, and Mama Ev go home, while John-Two, Lo-Tone, and I head over to Charlie's Little Grocery Store for coffee and frozen peas.

The three of us walk side by side up the hill toward Lee Street. Lo-Tone flips his baseball from his hand, bounces it off his forearm, and catches it—another one of his coordination-improvement drills. "Good heavens," he says. "I think Della Tillborn is sweet on somebody. I merely suspected it before, Mr. Banks, but now I'm sure of it."

My stomach clinches. "You think?"

"I don't think—that's your spesh-ee-AL-i-tee. I *know*," says Lo-Tone. Flip, bounce, catch. "How could anyone miss the way she was eyeing me up through the whole service?" Flip, bounce, catch. Flip, bounce, catch. I glance over at John-Two, and he just shrugs. "Mmmm hmmmm . . . the girl's got eyes for the Tone."

I think he's yanking my chain, but I'm not sure. Best thing to do, I decide, is change the subject. I turn to John-Two. "So, what did you think of the service?" I ask.

"It was fine. Reverend Johnson knows how to do it right. Never goes too long, doesn't go too short, and he's always smooth."

"Yeah, he's pretty cool, man," I say nervously.

I don't know why I'm so nervous. This walk, I think, is a good time to talk to him about my plan. If there is anyone in the world who can give me advice and support on handling Dad, it's John-Two.

"You all right?" he asks.

"Oh, me? Yeah, I'm all right. Just thinkin'." What if he thinks it's a stupid idea? What if he thinks I'm a goof for wanting to go? But we've only got a couple of more blocks to go, and time's short. I've got to do it now.

"You know?" says Lo-Tone. He stops his ball flipping and looks serious. "That march that Mrs. Carter was talking about? That sounds like it might be a good deal. Trip to Washington, see the capital, do a little demonstratin'? Could be fun."

As usual, Lo-Tone has come out with just what I want to say while I'm still stuck thinking about it. "That's right!" I shout, probably a little too loudly, because both John-Two and Lo-Tone stop and stare at me. "I mean, I was thinking the same thing!" I turn to face John-Two and blurt my thoughts out in one long string of words. "I want to go with the church to the march on Washington, I mean, I *really* want to go, I've got the money in savings, so I can afford to go, so what do you think?"

"Take it easy, little brother. The first question has to be, what is *Dad* going to think?"

"You think I don't know that? Don't answer a question with a question," I say. "I wanna know what *you* think." I look him dead in the eyes with as much intensity as I can muster. "I want to be like you and your friends and make a difference. Stand up and be heard. I figure that this is my chance, that this is a start. So, what do you think?"

"I think it's cool," he says, and a smile forms. "You don't need to be like me and my friends, or Dad, Grandpa Will, Mama Ev, Mom, or anybody else. You just need to be yourself. The brother I know and trust. The level-headed kid who I know will think of a good way to get Dad to go along with what you believe in."

"Thanks," I say, and in my head I'm about as proud of myself as I've ever been. There's nothing cooler than having your older brother tell you that, well, you're OK to hang around with.

"This is fantastic!" says Lo-Tone. "We'll be there together. Maybe I'll ask Della if she wants to go." Flip, bounce, catch. He's been working lefty. Now he switches to his right side. He's not as good on the right, and the ball glances off his arm and rolls into the street and down the hill that we've just climbed. He runs back to snag it.

"Are you going to be there in Washington?" I ask John-Two.

"I don't think I'm going. I'll be at a meeting in Chicago that weekend with some SNCC dudes. They're thinking about changing their approach, breaking away to do things another way."

"What do you mean?"

"They don't think we're militant enough."

"You mean, kick some butt?" I ask, excited.

John-Two looks at me and shakes his head. "Man, this is serious. Little brother, you know I've been down with the passive resistance ideology for a while. Now I'm beginning to wonder if it's working. We're getting our behinds whipped down South by the Klan and everybody else who thinks we're Communist dupes out to destroy America. I've been punched, sprayed with water, hit in the head with a billy club, and even had a close friend killed. Between you and me, I'm sick of it."

I've never heard John-Two talk like this. Earlier in the day, he was so sure that he was doing the right thing with the nonviolence.

"So what are trying to say?"

"What I'm trying to say is that . . . "

"What?"

He looks at me as though he's deciding whether to continue. Finally, he says, "I might be wrong. Maybe we *should* hit back."

Now that John-Two is saying it, it seems more real.

And suddenly, I see how scary real can be. "They've got guns," I say. "You could get killed."

John-Two nods. "I know. I know. I'm not going to do anything drastic—for now at least. But I want to hear what these brothers have to say. I'm starting to lose my faith in this whole nonviolence thing. Not about the outcome—freedom—just the methods. You understand?"

"I don't know if I do or if I don't. Would you really sacrifice yourself? Or could you really hurt somebody else?"

John-Two looks thoughtful, then nods his head. "All right, little brother, I hear you."

Lo-Tone catches back up with us, panting. He starts up again with his righty drill. Flip, bounce, catch. Flip, bounce—the ball ricochets off Lo-Tone's arm again, but this time it bonks me on the side of the head.

"Geez, Coleman," I say. I snatch the ball from the ground and shove it in my suit-jacket pocket. "Give it a rest, will ya?"

Lo-Tone looks hurt. "Hey, sorry, man." The three of us walk on silently, listening to the birds and to the click of our shoes against the sidewalk. My opinion of John-Two hasn't changed, but I see now that even he isn't always sure what the right thing is. But he's still my brother and the smartest guy I know. I don't know if I accept the new "method," but it's beginning to seem as though things are a little more complicated than I realized. And now the feeling I had in church about the march—that feeling of being sure—is wavering. I know I'm a little scared of what Dad's going to say about it, but now it seems that part of me *wants* him to say no. What's wrong with me?

We get to Charlie's and go inside. John-Two goes to the freezer case in search of the peas. Lo-Tone, of course, heads straight for the candy counter and starts feeling the packs of baseball cards. I grab a can of Chock Full o' Nuts, Dad's favorite, and join Lo-Tone. I look over his shoulder. I'm still feeling bad about snapping at him, but he's as clear as a glass of spring water on a hot summer day and has already washed it away. He's got a pack of cards in each hand, and his eyes are closed. "I feel it," he says. "In one of these packs is the elusive Willie Mays." That's Lo-Tone, my mystical friend. He's actually pretty lucky with the cards. He's got one of the best collections I've ever seen. "Here it is," he says, holding up the pack in his left hand. He puts the other one back in the rack.

We pay for our purchases and go back outside. Lo-Tone rips open the pack and riffles through the cards. "Ernie Banks, Moe Thacker, Brian McCall," he mutters. "Ooh—Jim Bouton, another Joe Pepitone, Ron Santo, Carl Yastrzemski, Louis Aparicio—cool!" He quickly flips through the rest. "No Willie. Dang!"

"Tough luck," I say.

"Yeah." He puts the cards into his pocket and shoves the bubble gum into his mouth. "I gotta get going. You want to play some whiffleball after dinner?" Lo-Tone asks me.

"Sure," I say. "Come by my house about four-thirty."

Lo-Tone lopes down the street.

As soon as he's out of sight, John-Two turns to me. "Look, Clayton, I'm just tired. I still believe in what we're doing with SNCC. You get me?"

"Yeah."

"You mad at me?"

"I just wish you were going to Washington."

"I know."

We walk silently for another minute or so. Then John-Two asks, "You want me to talk to Dad about you going to Washington?"

I want to say yes, but I know that if I'm going to do this, I have to do it myself. I've got to make Dad understand where I'm coming from.

I shake my head no, and for no reason I tag John-Two in the arm and haul my behind as fast as I can back to Grandma and Grandpa's house.

"Oh, chump, you're mine when I get you!" John-Two yells, laughing and running behind me.

Chapter 6

I love summer. St. Louis in the summer is like a steam bath—98° in the shade, 98 percent humidity, and 9,800 mosquitoes dive-bombing my head.

John-Two and I bound into the house, and I go straight to my room to change out of my church clothes. My doubts have lifted, and I'm red-hot with the prospect of going to Washington. I don't know exactly what to expect there. In fact, I don't know what to expect at all. But I feel that this trip to Washington will give me the answers I'm looking for.

And John-Two's encouragement has given me confidence. I'm so confident, in fact, that a visit to the Tillborns' seems like the best idea in the world. Now that I'm going to the march, I feel I have something interesting to say to Della, something to push the image of me as the dope with the spewing ketchup bottle out of her mind. I can worry about straightening it out with Dad later.

When I go downstairs, John-Two sits at the kitchen table while Dad makes a fresh pot of coffee. "Where are you off to?" Dad asks.

"I thought I'd take a walk down to Dr. Tillborn's and see if he and E.J. are in the mood for some hoops."

"Is that right?" my dad says with a sly grin.

"And if Della happens not to be there, can we expect you right back?" says John-Two.

"Very funny."

"Don't overstay your welcome," Dad says. "And tell the Tillborns I said hello."

"I will . . . I mean, I won't, and I will," I say.

I can hear chuckling as I run out the door.

I've always liked to play basketball with Dr. Tillborn and E.J., but since E.J. went off to college a couple years ago, and I got busier with sports and school, we don't have as many chances to play. But E.J. is home for the summer, and we've managed to get a few good games in. More important, I'm fairly successful in my attempts to impress Della on the court. I'll hit the occasional 20-foot jumper or win one of our games of HORSE. Sometimes she'll look out of the kitchen window, which overlooks their backyard, where the hoop is. She'll sit there with her mother, Sara Mae, a sweet and wonderful mother who makes the most delicious blueberry pie you can imagine. Mrs. Tillborn also used to be the terror of eighth-grade math students. The kids called her Airborne

Tillborn because she'd swoop into the classroom bearing pop-quizzes and tests, causing hearts to beat faster and the brains of the weak and unprepared to melt. And out of kindness, or maybe pity, she retired the year before I was to have her.

Anyway, Della occasionally sits with her mom out on the back steps and reads while I work on my jump shot with her brother and father. I sometimes see her peeking over her book. At least I think she peeks.

Unfortunately, it's when she says something directly to me that I make a fool of myself.

"Good shot, Clayton," she'll say.

"Uh."

So today, on my walk over, I practice what to say.

I hit a 20-foot jumper. No backboard. No rim. All net.

"Great shot, Clay," says Della.

"Thanks, Della, and might I add that is a lovely dress you have on."

"Oh, Clay, you really think so?"

"Why, yes. It matches the ribbon in your hair."

"Oh, Clay, will you sit on the porch with me and have a glass of lemonade?"

"It would be my pleasure." I offer the crook of my muscular arm, she puts her own delicate limb through, and I escort her to the porch swing.

When I get to the Tillborns', I'm surprised to see Dr. Tillborn and E.J. in the driveway. Dr. Tillborn puts a cooler in the trunk, and E.J. holds four fishing poles.

"Hello, Clay," Dr. Tillborn greets me as I walk up the driveway.

"Hey, Dr. T.," I say. "I came over to see if you were up for some basketball. But I see you've got other plans."

"Tomorrow night's the full moon, and a change in the weather's coming. They should be biting like crazy today. Care to join us? We're just going over to Lake George."

"Well, I'm not much for fishing—" and I'm about to finish my polite refusal when Della walks out the front door, her face shaded by a big straw hat. She wears blue jeans rolled up to midcalf, and a big white shirt with red stripes tied around her middle. She carries a tackle box. "—but what the heck? It might be fun!" I finish.

"Hi, Clayton," says Della with a warm smile as she hands the tackle box to her dad. "Did I hear right? Are you coming along?"

E.J. looks her up and down. "Dang, Della. How many times do I have to tell you not to wear my shirts?"

"Oh, please, E.J.! I don't want to get any of mine all fishy."

"So you grab one of my favorites? What about the blue checked one?"

"Eeeww, that ugly thing?"

I can't imagine a burlap sack looking ugly on Della.

"Dad," says E.J.

"Dellamanda."

"E.J., please. I promise I'll wash it *and* iron it when I'm done with it."

E.J. is softening. How could he not? "And the one I'm wearing."

"OK."

"And the one I wore to church."

"Dad!"

Dr. T. raises his hands. "This is between you two."

"Oh . . . all right," she says with a mock pout. She looks at me. "Clayton, you'll need a hat. The sun reflecting off the water sure can strain your eyes. I'll go find one."

"Uhhh," I say.

I watch her walk up to the front door. What am I thinking? I can hardly get a whole sentence out right when I'm around her, and now I've agreed to spend the whole afternoon with her—fishing! I'm a terrible fisherman. Oh, well, she's a girl, so I won't look that bad next to her. I just hope I can avoid making a fool of myself compared to E.J. and Dr. Tillborn.

"Banks!" Dr. Tillborn is saying my name loudly.

"Oh, sir, sorry—thanks."

"Thanks, what? I asked if you'd like to tell your dad you're going with us."

"Oh, yes," I say. "I'll run home and run right back."

"As I said, Clayton, you run home and wait for us. We'll pick you up on the way out of town."

"Oh, great. Sure. Good idea."

My feet are a blur as I fly down the sidewalk. When I get home, I find John-Two sitting on the front porch.

"That was a quick game," says John-Two as I bound up the porch steps.

"Where's Dad?" I say.

"Inside. What's got you all in an uproar?"

"The Tillborns invited me to go fishing."

John-Two just laughs. "I'd love to see this. Can I come too?"

"Buzz off." I run into the house. Dad's in the den reading a book.

"Dad, can I go fishing with the Tillborns?"

Dad puts down his book, slow as can be, and just as slowly reaches for his coffee cup, takes a sip, and puts it back. I'm jumping from one foot to another, and he doesn't even notice.

"Will you be home for dinner?"

"Um—I don't know. I forgot to ask."

"Well, you know how we feel about Sunday dinner in this family, and John-Two hasn't been home for a visit in so long."

"Dad, please."

He looks at me. "I don't know. . . ."

John-Two walks in. "Let him go, Dad. I've had my fill of his goofy face for one day anyway."

Dad smiles. "All right, son. Just be careful."

"Yeah, be careful you don't knock Della's pretty straw hat in the water," says John-Two.

"How do you know—?"

"They're in the driveway waiting for you."

"Get a move on," Dad says. "We'll try to save a plate for you."

"Thanks!'

"But no promises!"

"OK!" I run out of the house and down the driveway.

Della stands next to the open back door. "Sorry, Clayton, but I get the window seat," she says with a mischievous grin.

"That's OK," I say, climbing in next to E.J. "I like the middle. Hi, Mrs. Tillborn."

"Hello, Clay. It's nice that you're joining us."

Soon we're out on the interstate and leaving the suburbs behind. It doesn't take long before I realize how different the Tillborns are from my family. There's a lot of talking, just like at the Banks house. But what's talked about—that's where the differences come in. With us it's discussing and debating. With the Tillborns, it's good-natured teasing, joking, and storytelling and lots of laughter. While the miles go by, I just sit back, relax, and enjoy the scenery. Not to mention the light touch of Della's leg against mine. It's turning out to be a surprisingly wonderful day.

"You do much fishing?" E.J. asks me.

"No, not much."

"That's good, then. Della will have company while she's *not* catching fish."

"You wish," Della cries. "Care to put your money where your mouth is?"

"Oh, little sister, I can't take your allowance again. I just wouldn't feel right."

She turns to me. "He's scared. You stay with me, and I'll show you how it's done."

"I might need more than just a few tips," I say. "I think I'll need some lessons."

"It will be my pleasure," she says with that cat-eyed smile that makes me all woozy.

We get to the entrance to the state park and wait while the cars ahead of us pass through the gate. When it's our turn, the park ranger, a skinny red-faced man, bends down to look into the car.

"Where ya'll coming from?" he asks in a deep Ozark drawl.

"Middlefield," says Dr. Tillborn, with a polite smile.

"So ya'll fixin' to do some fishin'?"

"Yes. I figure the conditions are optimal for a fast bass bite."

"Optimal? Is that so?" He nods thoughtfully. "You fixing to stay long? Overnight?"

"No, just for the afternoon," Dr. Tillborn says.

The ranger still peers into the car. I notice he has one crooked top front tooth that sticks out between his lips even when his mouth is closed. I decide he looks like Ollie, the dragon puppet from TV. He and Dr. Tillborn look at each other, Dr. Tillborn still smiling, still polite, still patient. "Do ya'll have everything you need? Bait, tackle, and all?"

"Sure do, we're all set," Dr. Tillborn says.

"OK, then. That'll be a dollar," says the park ranger.

Dr. Tillborn hands him a dollar and takes the yellow day sticker.

"Ya'll take care of yourselves, you hear?" says the park ranger.

"We will." Dr. Tillborn glances over his shoulder at

E.J. as he drives away from the entrance gate. "Think we should start at the rocks, or the willows?"

"Rocks. Definitely. Save the willows for when the shadows hit later this afternoon."

"Good thinking."

I don't listen to the rest of the conversation. I'm occupied wondering whether cars full of white people get the once-over like we did. But the Tillborns don't seem bothered, so maybe I'm overreacting.

But when we get to the parking area, I'm not so sure. We're the only blacks, and I can feel the stares. I'm amazed that the Tillborns aren't paying any attention. They're laughing, joking, teasing, just like always, as we unload the car.

"Here, Clayton," says Dr. Tillborn, handing me a fishing pole. "have you ever used a bait caster before?"

"No," I say, examining the shiny black reel with its gears and knobs. I've never even seen one before. Banks-style fishing is off the pier with a bamboo pole, a hunk of cheese on a hook, and a bobber.

"Della will show you how," he says.

"It's easy," she says.

"Clay, why don't you help me with this?" says Mrs. Tillborn and hands me a big beach blanket, an umbrella, and two folding chairs. "I'm afraid I'm more interested in comfort than in fish. I'll be sitting in a pretty spot on the shore with my pole in the water and a nice novel on my lap, and if a fish happens to come along and bite my hook, then that's fine. If not, I've just had a pleasant day in the sunshine."

Dr. Tillborn smiles and pats his wife's arm. "I don't know where she gets these crazy notions. Certainly not from me."

We trudge down the gravel road to the lake with our gear, find a spot, and set Mrs. Tillborn up under her umbrella. I follow the rest of the Tillborns down the shore toward the rocks. E.J. and Dr. Tillborn immediately start casting. Their bait—big, jointed lures in the shape of fat fish with lots of hooks—goes whizzing out over the water and lands with a smooth *plip!*

That can't be too hard, I say to myself.

"OK, Clay, here's what you do," Della says, getting ready to demonstrate with her rod. "You're right handed? Then hold the rod in your right hand, like this, with your thumb on the reel, here." She puts her thumb on the spool of fishing line. "You flip this little lever over to release the spool so line can go out. Got it so far?"

"Sure."

"Then you bring the rod back over your shoulder, pitch it forward, and let go of the spool. To stop the spool, you put your thumb back down on it. Watch now." And she goes through the motion and zings her lure out into the water. It doesn't go quite as far as her dad's and brother's, but it enters the water with the same smooth *plip!*

"Are you ready to try?"

"I guess so."

I swing the rod back, flip it forward, lift my thumb, and the lure smacks into the water about a foot in front of me. "Ugh," I say.

"That's OK," says Della. "You just forgot to release the bale. Try again."

This time, I pitch the rod forward and the lure goes a little farther, but it hits the water with a crash that I'm sure has scared away every fish within a mile.

"OK, not bad for a first try," Della says. "Try keeping your thumb off the spool for just a second longer. Stop it just when it's entering the water."

Oh, boy. It's slowly sinking in that Della knows what she's doing out here, and if I'm going to enjoy myself at all, I have to get used to taking pointers from a girl. "I got it," I say. "Just a second longer." I wind up and cast. The lure goes sailing smoothly out over the water, but before I get my thumb down, the spool spins out of control. The next thing I know, the smooth spool has become a tangled ball of fishing line.

"Uh oh. A backlash," Della says.

"What happened?" I cry, horrified at the tangled mess in my hand.

"You put your thumb down just a little too late. The lure hit the water and stopped, but the spool kept spinning offline. What you have to do now is pull the line off till the tangle is straightened out, and then reel it all back in."

"What a mess," I say.

"No big deal. It happens to all of us once in a while. You just have to get the timing down. You'll get the hang of it."

I work on untangling my line while Della takes a few casts. *She makes it look easy,* I think. *What can she be thinking of me?* I get the line straightened out and plant my feet for another cast. I notice she's not watching, and I appreciate that. I wind up and pitch. This time the lure sails out over the water. I watch it carefully and put my thumb down on the spinning spool just as the lure makes contact with the water.

Plip!

"Good job!" Della says. "Now catch a fish." She lays her hand on my arm and smiles. "I want my dad and E.J. to know I'm a good teacher."

Della and I stand about 15 feet apart and move down the shoreline casting our bait. She tells me about some of the places she's fished with her dad and some of the fish she's caught. I can see she really loves fishing. I just listen, happy to be out there by the lake with her, listening to her talk. It feels so comfortable, and all the awkwardness I usually feel around her has gone away. Every once in a while, she gives me a pointer—reel slower, cast close to the edge of the weeds, stuff like that—and I do what she says, but I don't feel desperate to catch a fish, though it would be a great way to score points with her.

"Ooh!" she says and jerks back on her rod. It bends and then suddenly straightens out, and line starts to peel off her reel.

"Do you have a fish? Do you have a fish?" I yell.

"Yes, and it's big!" she yells back.

She just stands there while the fish runs away with her line.

I reel in and run up next to her. "What are you going to do?"

"Wait till it gets tired, and reel it in."

Sure enough, the line stops, and she reels in. There's a swirl on top of the water and I see the fish's tail, then her reel starts buzzing again as the fish speeds away.

Della laughs. "I think it's a big carp!" She fights it for a few minutes, patiently reeling the fish in and then letting it take line out. "Gosh, my arm is getting tired," she says. "I'm not gonna be able to keep this up much longer." I can see how hard she struggles to keep the end of the rod up out of the water when the fish is pulling, but she's holding her own. Finally, the pulling gets less and less. "Here he comes," she says as the fish comes into sight in the shallow water. She reels it in close and picks it up by the gill.

"Oooh whee, that's ugly," I say.

"Ugly?" she says. "I never thought of them as ugly. It's just a carp. They taste good."

Looking at the thick scales, the sucking mouth, and the fleshy thing dangling from its lip, I try to think of something I'd be less eager to put in my mouth, and I can't think of a thing. "How much do you think it weighs?" I ask.

"Maybe eight pounds."

"Where are you going to put it?"

"Right on this stringer," she says, taking a plastic cord from her jeans pocket. She strings the fish, ties the other end of the stringer around a stick, and puts the fish back into the water.

"Mercy me, chile, you have brought us quite a catch,"

65

Mrs. Tillborn says as Della and I walk up with our stringer of fish. I caught a small bass, and Della caught three more besides her carp.

"Dad and E.J. aren't back yet?" Della says.

"No, but I expect they'll be along soon. They'll be getting hungry," says Mrs. Tillborn.

"We'll wait for them before we eat," says Della. "But we could sure use a soda." She opens up the cooler. "Nehi?"

"Yes!" I say, and sit down on the blanket next to Mrs. Tillborn's chair. "Did you catch anything?"

"Shhh," she whispers to me behind her hand. "I haven't had my hook in the water all day." In full voice, she says, "No, darn it, not a bite."

"Tough luck," I say with a wink.

E.J. and Dr. Tillborn walk up. They have a stringer of fish too. "Looks like we all had some luck," Dr. Tillborn says. He looks at our stringer. "Clay, do we have you to thank for that magnificent carp?"

"No, mine is that little bass next to it."

"Oh, that's fine," he says. "That's sweet meat."

The men sit down, and Mrs. Tillborn starts unpacking food from the cooler: ham sandwiches, leftover fried chicken, potato salad, peanut butter cookies. It's a real feast.

"Wow," I say, taking it all in.

"Well don't just gawk. Dig in," says Dr. Tillborn.

I grab a drumstick and some potato salad.

"Looks like you got yourselves a right fine banquet going on."

We all look up to see where the comment came from. Two white boys, maybe a few years older than Della and I, glare down on us from a rise behind us.

None of us says anything.

"I'll say," says the other one.

"We have plenty," says Dr. Tillborn. "You're welcome to share."

I look at him in astonishment.

"We don't eat no coon food," says the other one, and they laugh.

"Sara Mae," Dr. Tillborn says, "could you please pass me a napkin?"

"Me too," says E.J. And the Tillborns continue on with their meal as though nothing is unusual.

What is going on here? I'm thinking. *Isn't anybody going to say anything?*

The boys are still there, staring at us. And I'm the only one looking at them. And I can't take it any longer.

I stand up. "What are you looking at?" I demand.

"Near as I can figure, I'm lookin' at a bunch a Negrahs where they ain't got no bidnis bein'," says the tall one.

"Clay," Della says softly.

"We got as much right to be here as anyone," I say.

"Clayton!" Dr. Tillborn barks. "Sit down." I look at him. He's glaring at me with almost as much intensity as the kids up on the hill. I don't move.

"Right now," he says. I look back up at the kids and then at Dr. Tillborn again. I'm trapped, defeated. I sit down.

"Face the water," says Dr. Tillborn. I turn, and now my back is to the kids. "Move along, young men," he says to the boys, and to me, "Now would you like another Nehi, Clay?"

"No thank you," I mutter.

"You can pass me one," says E.J.

"Grape or orange?" says Dr. Tillborn, peering into the cooler.

"Orange sounds good."

I look up over my shoulder just in time to see one of the boys heave a big handful of grass with a clod of dirt attached. It lands square on top of the cooler. I jump up, ready to—well, I don't know what, but I don't have a chance to find out because E.J. clamps his big hand on my shoulder and pushes me down. The boys turn and run away, whooping and laughing.

There's a silent pause, but only for the length of a heartbeat. "So tell us how you landed that big carp, Della," Dr. Tillborn says as he tosses the clump aside and brushes the dirt off the cooler with his napkin.

"Mom, did you bring any potato chips?" E.J. asks.

"Sure did. They're in the basket."

"Believe it or not, it was on a plastic worm," says Della.

"I'll be."

And that's the way the rest of the day goes, and the ride home too—the Tillborns carrying on in their happy-go-lucky way as if nothing ever happened, and me completely unable to shake those ignorant white boys and their filthy dirt clod off my mind.

Dr. Tillborn stops in front of my house, and I jump out of the car.

"Bye, Clay," Della says. "I had a really nice time. You're a good fisherman."

"Thanks," I reply. "Thank you for taking me, Dr. Tillborn, Mrs. Tillborn." I realize I'm being stiff, but I can't help it.

"We'll have to do it again, really soon," says Dr. Tillborn.

"Yes," says Della.

"Thank you," I say and head up the front walk.

It's not late, but I'm hoping Dad and John-Two are in their rooms, and I can sneak up to mine without having to talk. No such luck. They're both in the kitchen. But from the expressions that greet me, I can tell they've been having one of their disagreements.

"How was fishing?" my Dad asks.

"Fine," I say. "How was dinner?"

"You know your grandmother," says Dad. "There's a plate in the refrigerator."

"I'm not really hungry," I say. "I'm pretty tired, in fact. I guess I'll go to bed."

"Lo-Tone came by," says John-Two.

"Dang! I forgot all about him," I say.

"We assuaged his grief with a bowl of Mama Ev's rice pudding," Dad says dryly.

As I trudge up the stairs, Dad and John-Two resume

their discussion. I know how Dad feels about eavesdropping, but I can't help it.

"I don't see the difference," John-Two says. "I'm working directly for what I believe in, not letting it be a side effect of some career pursuit."

"Side effect?" Dad spits out. "You make it sound as though pursuing a career is an illness, something to be avoided. Your cause will be advanced when you have pride in who you are. When you care enough about yourself to make something of your life, to develop the talents God gave you—that's how you'll advance your cause."

"There are so many ways that that's naive, I don't even know where to start," says John-Two.

"Oh, now I'm naive."

"I'm sorry Dad," John-Two says. "I just think you're underestimating the obstacles that exist for us to 'make something of our lives.' Besides, I don't see where working for a cause I feel passionately about is *not* developing my God-given abilities."

"By being a troublemaker?"

"Troublemaker." John-Two repeats the word as though it's wounded him. "Is that all you see?"

"I'm not interested in seeing my boy becoming a street fighter, or something worse, and then hide all the violence and hatred and destruction behind some notion that he calls a *cause*. You're just going to lose what people like me and your grandfather have gained."

John-Two's voice is flat. "So now you're making me

the enemy."

"You said it, not me."

I can't take any more of this. I tiptoe up to my room, strip my clothes off, and climb into bed. It's barely even dark out, and I watch the sky through my window turn from deep blue to black. I'm as far from sleep as I can be. Before long, a brightness begins to grow at the edge of my window. I sit up and lean over to see what it is. It's Mr. Tillborn's full moon, brilliant and shiny as a silver dollar. "You shine for us all, right?" I say softly. "You shine for me as much as for anyone. You're shining right into my room." I lie back and watch the moon inch across my window. Then it disappears and reappears a little while later in the other window. Clouds begin to pass, their edges glowing with moonlight until they darken the moon completely and then scuttle past, liberating the brightness. Soon, there are more clouds than moon. I'm thinking about everything and nothing—the disappointment I feel in the Tillborns, sadness over my Dad and John-Two not being able to agree. Excitement about taking my first steps, doubt about what Dad will say. Finally, these thoughts relax their stranglehold, and I drift off to sleep.

Sometime in the night I become aware of thunder crashing and lightning flashing, and I dream that there's a war in Wilson Park. I'm trying to knock a gun out of a man's hand with a baseball bat, but the bat is so heavy I can barely lift it. The gun fires and I'm shot. I feel no pain, only breathlessness. I know I'm weak. I don't remember dreaming after that.

Chapter 7

The day starts soggy, rainy, dark, and hot, and it fits my mood. Dad and John-Two aren't too cheerful at breakfast, which also suits me. The three Bankses munch their toast in gloomy silence.

Dad breaks it. "What have you got planned for today?" he asks me.

"Nothing special."

"Practice?"

"No. Tomorrow," I say.

"Just going to take it easy, then?"

"I guess so."

Dad and John-Two leave, Dad for the office, John-Two for who knows where. I turn on the radio while I do the dishes. That takes about three minutes. I walk from room to room, look in the refrigerator even though I'm not hungry, eat peanut butter out of the jar with my finger. I sit down in the living room, open a magazine I've already read, think about finding Lo-Tone, decide I'm not in the mood. Then I wander out the back door. Maybe I'll take a bike ride. I go to the shed and pull my bike out. The back tire is flat, so I start pushing it—the tire going thwop . . . thwop . . . thwop—to the service station down the block to fill it up.

After I fill it, I jump on. Hissssss—it's flat again. I kneel down and spin the tire. I see why—a little nail is jammed in between the treads. *OK then,* I say to myself, *that's the way it's going to be today.* The bike shop is about 13 blocks away, but what's the difference? I've got nothing to do. I walk my bike along the sidewalk, focusing on the thwop . . . thwop . . . thwop. It's starting to drizzle just as I reach the shop.

The clerk tells me it'll be a couple hours before they can fix the flat. I tell him I'll be back later and start walking home. The rain pours harder now, fat heavy drops that seem to explode when they hit the pavement. People walking down the street start to walk faster. If they have an umbrella, they open it. If they have a newspaper, they hold it over their head. I've got nothing. I'm getting soaked to the skin, but I'm enjoying it. I'm tough. What's a little rain, after all?

"Hey, Clay!" a girl's voice calls out behind me. I know right away it's Della. I pretend not to hear and keep walking. I just can't deal with her right now.

"Clay!" she yells louder. I turn the corner. It's not going to work. Footsteps are gaining on me. She catches up to me, laughing. "Clay, you must have water in your ears. I've been calling your name." She looks cute in a yellow raincoat and hat under her red umbrella. "Get under here. You're soaked." She lifts the umbrella over my head.

"I'm fine," I say.

We walk a few steps, Della close to me. "My mom says you'll have to come over for a fish fry."

"I don't like fish."

"You don't?"

"No."

"You didn't mention it yesterday."

"I didn't want to be rude."

"I thought everybody liked fish."

"Well, I don't."

Della bumps into me a little as we walk. "It's really OK," I say. "You don't have to share your umbrella. I'm soaked to the skin already, anyway."

"It's nice to share."

"You know," I persist. "Sorry. It's just that it's a little crowded."

"Oh," Della looks surprised, then confused. I can't meet her eyes and slide mine away. She takes a step away from me and walks along next to me sideways. "Are you all right?"

"Sure," I say. "I'm just in a hurry, kind of." I start to walk faster. I hear her footsteps stop.

"See you around?" she calls.

I turn. "Sure, sounds good."

Back home, I change into dry clothes and hang my wet ones in the bathroom. Then I go out on the front porch and sit. Seems like sitting is what I do best nowadays.

Tuesday morning is still gloomy, but the ground is dry. John-Two and I mow the lawn—he pushes and I rake up the clippings. Then we have lunch together.

"When are you going to get around to asking Dad about the march?" he asks. "Time's wastin'."

"Soon as I get the nerve, find the words, whatever."

"You've been a little down the past couple days," he says. "Ever since your outing with the Tillborns."

"Yeah," I say.

John-Two gives me the *Well?* look, but I can't talk about it. Instead I ask, "Have you been thinking any more about . . . ?" I don't know how to express it.

"Fighting fire with fire?"

"Yeah."

"I've been thinking about it a lot," John-Two says.

I give him the *Well?* look.

"I don't have any answers."

"I'm starting to think that it's the only way things are going to change."

"What's going on, little brother?"

"Why *should* they change, the people who want to keep us down? Even the people who don't hate us— what's in it for them to share what they have with us? And if they won't share voluntarily, they're going to have to be forced."

"There are more and more people thinking like that," says John-Two. "They're saying that if it's our right to have it, it's our right to take it. Whatever *it* is."

"Exactly. And when somebody's trying to keep you from doing something that you have every right to do, you have to stand up and fight."

"Good heavens, little brother, you *have* been thinking," John-Two says with a chuckle. "But I'm not sure you should lay all this on Dad right away."

"I know. I heard you two the other night. But he *has* to see. Maybe if we both explain it . . . "

Now John-Two laughs. "Oh, wow, little brother, you've got a lot to learn about the ways of the world. And you better start with Dad."

It's good to talk with John-Two. He always makes me feel less like a lonely spaceman, and I'm able to go to baseball practice with a lighter heart.

Mama Ev has never made a dinner that couldn't be described as perfect. Tuesday's is no exception. Check this out: lamb shanks with green peas, mashed potatoes, fresh garden salad with Italian dressing, and lemonade. That's not all. Apple pie. Freshly baked apple pie. Is there anything in the English language that sounds better than "freshly baked apple pie"?

When our family gets together for dinner, it's a yak-fest. Politics, religion, sports, rocket science—everybody has an opinion; everybody has something to say. I join in most times, except today. While Dad and Mama Ev gang up on Grandpa Will and John-Two about who was the greatest home-run hitter of all-time—Josh Gibson, Babe Ruth, or Roger Maris—I think about ways to tell Dad that I want to go to Washington. One hundred different scenarios go through my head during dinner, and all of them end with Dad saying, "No, you're not going— period. That's it. That's final!"

After dinner, I help Mama Ev with the dishes. It's a tradition. She washes, I wipe, and we talk. It's our time together. Dad, Grandpa Will, and John-Two are out on the porch talking about baseball. Or is it politics now? My mind, however, is still wondering and worrying.

"So, Junebug, what do you think Cinderella should wear to the ball?" Mama Ev asks as we wash dishes.

"Babe Ruth," I answer. "Wait a minute. What did you ask me?"

"What's on your mind, babe?" Mama Ev asks.

"I don't know," I say, wiping off a knife. "Nothing. I guess."

"Clay. Come on now. You can't fool your grandma."

She's right. I'm no good at trying to keep my feelings hidden from Mama Ev.

"OK, I'll tell you. But you've got to keep this a secret."

"Cross my heart," she says, moving closer to me.

"I want to go to Washington, with the church, to the march."

Mama Ev looks at me with the kind of intensity she shows when she's absolutely serious.

"Are you sure you want to do this?" she says. "You

sure you want to go to the march?"

"Yep, Mama Ev. I want to go in the worst way. When Mrs. Carter announced it, I thought, 'That's it!' Do you know what I mean?"

Mama Ev cocks her head.

"First, don't say 'yep,' " she says. "The word is *yes*. And no, honey, I'm not surprised. You are my daughter's child. Do you have money to go to Washington? Do you need any money? I'm so excited for you. Child, I'd go, but you know how my back is. Oh, the stories you'll tell us, and the memories you'll have. . . . "

I listen in silence to Mama Ev go on and on. Sure, I'm happy that she's happy, but it isn't her approval that I need. I still have to get Dad to let me go. I keep drying dishes and nodding my head.

"Junebug, are you paying any sort of attention to me?" Mama Ev asks, laughing a bit. "I'm every bit as long-winded as your grandfather, but you really should at least pretend that you're paying attention."

"Mama Ev, I'm sorry. But I'm wondering what Dad is going to say. What do you think he's going to say? You know how much he worries. Now I'm about to ask him to go to Washington, to attend a march for a cause that he really doesn't agree with."

"He agrees with it," Mama Ev says. "There isn't a black man anywhere who doesn't ache for a better life."

I stop drying.

Mama Ev continues, thoughtfully, "It's just that your father is a proud man. And sometimes that pride gets in

the way of seeing what's right." Mama Ev cups my jaw
with her wet hands. "Deep down, your daddy knows that
what's right is having the door open for everyone."

Mama Ev and I finish the dishes, and so I sit down at
the kitchen table while she takes two cups from the
cupboard and the water jug from the refrigerator and sets
them on the table. She picks up an apple from the fruit
dish, pulls out a knife from the drawer, sits down, and
begins to cut the apple into six slices for the two of us. I
pour us both a drink. Mama Ev says an apple and a full
glass of water after a big meal settles the stomach.

"Well, Junebug, you're in a bit of a jam," she says
taking a bite from one of the slices.

"So what am I going to do?"

"First off, you're not going to go talk to your father
about this with a negative attitude. Am I right?"

"OK."

"Second, when you ask him, you have to be honest."

"Whaddya mean?" I say, biting into an apple slice.

"What do you mean, you mean? I mean that you have
to be honest about your feelings. You have to convince
your dad that you're right, and you can't get flustered.
That's about all I can tell you."

Sounds good, but I'm not so sure this is going to
work on my dad. I take a big gulp of water. "What do
you think Mom would say to me, if she were here?"

Mama Ev looks up at the ceiling, squints, then turns
to look at me.

"Junebug, you two—you and your mom—are a lot

alike. Don't get me wrong, there's a lot of her inside your brother too. But you and your mom are two peas in a pod. You both think before you leap. Sometimes you overthink your problems, but that's not too bad of a trait. Now to your question: What would your mother say right now? Clayton, I think she'd tell you to follow your heart, and that takes courage."

Once again, I know she's right. She's always right, except when she thinks that she knows more about baseball than I do.

I swallow the last bit of water from my cup, take the last apple slice, and give Mama Ev a peck on the cheek.

"Thanks," I say.

"Always here to help. When are you going to ask him?"

"No better time than the present," I say, walking out of the kitchen.

Dad, John-Two, and Grandpa Will are still out on the porch. Dad and Grandpa sit in rocking chairs reading different sections of the newspaper. John-Two sits on the top step. With that faraway look in his eyes, he slowly sips a tall glass of lemonade. Thinking about Mississippi, no doubt.

I sit down on the porch swing next to Dad and Grandpa. I figure that I'll start off with a little small talk.

"It sure has been hot lately, Dad."

"August in St. Louis is *always* hot."

Dad doesn't even look up. He just rocks and reads. I

look at John-Two, who smiles and gives me a thumbs up.

OK, here's try number two.

"So, Dad, what do you think about the Yankees this year? Think they'll win the World Series?"

To know my father is to know that he is quick when it comes to getting to the point. To know me is to know that I stink at small talk.

"Clayton, enough of this chitchat," he says. "What do you really want?"

Abrupt and to the point. That's my Dad.

I swallow, take a deep breath, and blurt it out. "Dad, you've always said I'm mature for my age. And I made good grades last year. I've got my own money. School doesn't start until September. I'm in good health. I'm in good spirits. So doesn't it seem logical that I should be able to go—with the church—to Washington, to the march?"

I end by exhaling, full of confidence that I have stated my case like Grandpa Will did before the school board. John-Two winks. Mama Ev is busy crocheting something for someone's new baby, her fingers moving as fast as her arthritis will allow. And Grandpa Will is just stunned.

Dad is on his feet. Not a good sign. There are two things my father does when he's convinced that he is right. First, he stands. Second, he takes on what John-Two and I call his preacher stance, in which he plants his feet about shoulder-width apart and leans his palms on the nearest available flat surface. Here comes the fire and brimstone. And here I stand, without any protection.

"Son, I thought that you would have better sense than to think . . . with all that's going on in this world . . . that I would let you traipse halfway across this continent to that . . . that . . . march. Who put you up to this?" he says, looking at John-Two.

"It wasn't me!" John-Two protests. "This was his idea. But if you ask me—"

"I *didn't* ask you."

Suddenly, everything starts to slow down and speed up at the same time. My heart is pounding, but my brain has completely shut off, abandoning me at my time of need. Mama Ev is setting the speed record for crocheting. Grandpa Will is still stunned, looking at us as if we are a bad act on *The Ed Sullivan Show*.

Dad slowly turns on his heel back to me. The preacher inside him is going for the conversion. He raises his hands heavenward.

"Boy, do you realize how hard I have to work? I can't go gallivanting across the country, leaving my patients, just 'cause some colored folk tryin' to tell the government what it needs to do. How responsible would it be for me to do that? Huh?"

At this, John-Two leaps to his feet, hisses something under his breath, throws up his arms, and storms out the porch door. Mama Ev shouts, "Don't slam the screen—" BAM! "—door."

He's gone. Dad doesn't flinch; he keeps right on talking. With sword flaming, he says, "I think it'll do more harm than good. I wouldn't dream of going!"

"*You* don't have to go, I *want* to go."

I meant to not say that out loud. Now I've done it. He's gone from preacher to avenging angel. "Oh, so now you're grown-up enough to talk smart?"

"No sir. I know how you feel, but why won't you listen to how I feel?"

The silence is so loud on that porch, I think my eardrums are about to burst. There is a look on my father's face that I've never seen before. And why is Mama Ev smiling? Grandpa Will has gone from shock to horror to surprise.

I can't stop now. So I go on. "I . . . I think the march will be good for me to attend. Why? Because it's about my future, my time. You talk a lot about what it was like for you growing up in the thirties and forties. But for me, I'm growing up in the sixties. I'll be working in the seventies and eighties. I want things to be better for me and my children. What was that Mom always said? 'If you aren't a part of the solution, then you might be part of the problem.' I don't want to be the problem. I want to be part of the solution. I have to go to Washington."

Now Grandpa Will speaks. "How can you argue with that, John?"

Dad sits down. Good sign. We've gone from red alert back to yellow. He sighs deeply. "I can't argue with that. I know you and John-Two think that I am a square. 'Out of it,' as you boys say. But I know what the world has done to our people. I've seen smart people get overlooked for jobs they were overqualified to do. I've had good friends who've had to leave the country—simply because they were Negroes—to practice the professions they were trained to do. I risked my life to prove that a Negro could fly an airplane in combat. In Europe, they told our allies that Negroes had tails and ate children. No march is going to change the hearts of people who would do such things."

This discussion is not going my way, and I begin to lose my cool. "You think that I don't know what prejudice is like just because you've kept me sheltered in Wilson Park where we all have it so good? You can't protect me forever. We're living in a different world from yours, Dad. I see things. I know things. We can't stay separate forever." It's so frustrating not to be heard, and I'm beginning to lose my train of thought. "I'm going!"

Dad is speechless. But just for a moment. And when he begins to talk, it's in a low, even tone, not much more than a whisper. I've heard that tone before, and I know immediately that I've gone too far.

"Well, Clayton, it seems as though you must have experienced a lot to have developed such awareness. So I can't see how going to this march is going to enrich you in any way. But now, you're a boy of fourteen, and I still have the right to make some decisions for you, and I'm deciding that you won't be going to this march. There'll be plenty of other marches, I suspect, in this changing world of yours, and you can go to as many as you want, when you're a man."

Lo-Tone has the most impeccable timing in the world.

"Hey, Banks! What's the good word?" he says, hopping over the picket fence.

Frozen faces greet him. No one says a word.

"It looks like it's *no,*" I say with venom.

"I will ignore that remark as the honest mistake of a rash and intemperate youth," my dad says.

"Hey, Clay, what about some kick-the-can?" Lo-Tone asks, with a silly grin on his face. "Petway and Augie and Sanford are out on Woodlawn."

"May I be excused, Dad?" I ask formally. I just want to get away from here.

"Yes, you may."

"I'll be home before ten," I say, hoping to sound responsible and grown up.

Dad says nothing, just gets up and walks into the house.

Grandpa Will looks shocked too. "He'll be all right, son," Grandpa Will says. "Least, I hope so."

"Why's everybody so glum?" Lo-Tone asks.

"Hush up and let's go," I say as I brush past him toward the fence. "Let's just go." I jump over.

If there is one thing about Lo-Tone, it's that when he realizes I'm serious about something, he generally lets me stew for a while. He'll just walk or sit or whatever, and let me brood until I say something. We walk briskly for a couple of blocks, until I stop.

"He may be able to stop me from going to the march, but he can't stop me from believing what I believe," I say.

"Oh, no," says Lo-Tone. "He's not letting you go? Why?"

"He says I'm not old enough. I don't know. It's just not what *he* believes in, so he thinks he has the right to dictate what I believe in."

"Oh, man, you've *gotta* go. I already paid my twenty bucks."

"What am I supposed to do, Lo-Tone?" I said. "You heard him: 'I will ignore that remark as the words of a rash and inexperienced young man.' "

"I think he said 'rash and intemperate youth.' "

"You're *no* help. You tryin' to make me feel worse?"

"I'm just trying to get you to lighten up."

"That's easy for you. You're going."

"I think you should just expect it to all work out and it will. That's what I do."

"I'm not you. Things don't just fall into place for me."

"Hey, there are the guys," Lo-Tone says, breaking into a trot. "Let's go kick some can."

I have to laugh at that in spite of my lousy mood.

Chapter 8

I've spent most of the week by myself, riding my bike and thinking about the march and Della and the big game. Mostly the big game. It seems to be the only thing that means anything to me that I have any control over. It's weird that Lo-Tone and I haven't seen each other since last Tuesday. Maybe he's keeping to himself too.

Dad and I aren't talking much. We're not giving each other the cold shoulder or anything; we're just limiting to it to "Good morning" and "Could you pass the sports section?" or "We're running low on milk." Mama Ev and Grandpa Will are the only people I've really talked to about anything this week. Even with them, the conversations have been short. But I learned they were as surprised as I was that Dad came down on me so hard about the march. They don't want to interfere, though. I guess I don't blame them; it probably wouldn't do any good anyway, stubborn as Dad can be.

It's Saturday, the afternoon of the championship game. While we're on the field warming up, the bleachers slowly fill. It seems as though all of Wilson Park is turning out for the game. Suddenly, I see Della, in a beautiful pink-and-white sun dress. Oh, man she's so . . . so . . . But then she sees me, and I turn away. My heart shrivels up. *It's best this way,* I tell myself.

The game seems to go our way from the beginning. We scored three quick runs in the first inning, and Lo-Tone would have a shut-out going except for a fifth-inning double that scored on an error. That's the good news. The bad news is that now, in the last inning, the bases are loaded, with only one out, and our opponent's best hitter, Lucius "Godzilla" Davis, is up next and moving slowly to the plate. He swings the bat so hard that when he's in the on-deck circle I can feel the breeze from his warm-up swings—not a good thing because I don't think he washes too well.

Facing Lo-Tone on the pitcher's mound, I say, through clenched teeth, "Could you please, next time, throw what I tell you to throw!"

The reason I'm irked is that Lo-Tone has just blown off my signal and thrown a curve that breaks so weakly it straightens out and stalls in midair, like a neglected tetherball on a pole. Thankfully, Tommy "The Other Godzilla" Higgins could only turn this gift into a Texas-league single, or it would be 3–2 now.

On the mound, Lo-Tone says to me, like he's Bob

Gibson or something, "Ah, man, I got this. I'm just tryin' to bring some drama to the game."

"You can't even spell *drama*! Look, 'Tone, just follow my signals and we'll be cool. I got people in the stands watching me, and you're making me look bad. OK?"

"OK, OK."

I start trotting back to the plate. Lo-Tone calls me back. "Hey, Clayton, your daddy change his mind yet about D.C.?"

"Lo-Tone, shut up and get ready."

I get back behind the plate.

"If it ain't my old pal, Claydene," says Lucius as he steps up to the plate. "I got a tissue in my pocket you can use to wipe your tears after I smack the ball over the fence."

I start to sniff the air, and draw my face up as though I've smelled a skunk.

"Lucius, I thought bath night at your house was last night. I think you missed it."

"Keep talkin', little man."

"Boys, I'm not going to have this," says Reverend Jenkins, the umpire. "I'm roastin' like a chicken back here. So let's play ball."

I get in my stance and flash one finger—fastball— and hit the right side of my mask to tell Lo-Tone to aim for the outside the plate. I figure Lucius will chase it.

Lo-Tone winds, stretches, fires. Pop! Right in the glove. Lucius doesn't chase. Ball one.

I look to the bench for a signal. Coach Carter shows

me fastball, low, inside. I nod. The crowd is loud and chanting for both teams. I see Dad, John-Two, Grandpa Will, and Mama Ev in the bleachers, carrying on as if they were cheering on the Cardinals. It still stings not to see Mom up there too.

I get ready to signal for a curveball. No, it was a fastball, low outside, right? Or not? I can't remember, but I can't look back at the coach again—he'll know my mind isn't on the game, and that's the one unforgivable sin on his team. I throw down two fingers for a curve. Lo-Tone kicks, fires, and tosses a ball that hits just in front of the plate. The ball brings up some dust, and I move my body in front of it to prevent it from getting away from me.

The crowd roars a collective "Oow." Lucius laughs out loud and steps out of the box. Two balls, no strikes. Coach yells time and signals me to join Lo-Tone and him on the mound.

"What in the name of ham fat is going on out here? What did you throw a curve for?"

"I didn't . . . That was Clayton's craziness!" Lo-Tone says.

With the evil look on my face, I shoot an arrow between Lo-Tone's eyes. "Sorry," I say to the coach.

"Sorry? You're going to be real sorry if you don't get in the game, son! Lo-Tone, give him a fastball, inside, just slow enough to jam him. Let's go for the double play."

"No, I think we can strike him out, Coach," I say defiantly.

"Clayton, this isn't a democracy. I don't care what you think. You've called a good game, but your inattention has been costly. Now do what I say."

"But coach . . . "

"You want to sit?"

"No, sir."

"Let's get this show on the road," the ump shouts.

Coach and I start to walk away.

"Clayton, I'm the coach. I've made the call."

"OK."

Not OK. I've been carrying this team all season long. The catcher is the brains of the team, right? My pitch-calling is what got us to the championship game. If it wasn't for me, we wouldn't be here.

I get behind the plate. Lucius is talkin' smack, and I'm not there. I'm in the zone. No, my boy is going to throw the curve. It's my call.

I show curve. Lo-Tone shakes it off. I show curve again. Lo-Tone shakes it off again.

"Ump, time," Coach Carter yells from the dugout. "I need to make a substitution. Clayton, get on over here and take off the gear!"

You can hear a pin drop. Instantly, I know that I've screwed up big time.

I take off my gear as fast as I can and give it to Gerald Vaughn. Gerry's not the best of players, but he can do one thing that I can't right now—be part of the team. He's been cheering from the bench the whole game, keeping score, and charting pitches. Whatever the team needs, he does.

Gerry trots out and takes his position behind the plate. He puts down one finger—fastball—and taps the inside part of his mask with his glove. Lo-Tone kicks and fires. Lucius turns on it and hits a chopper to Roland Jones, our shortstop. Jones tosses it to the second baseman, who tags the bag and then zings the ball to first for the double play to end the game. Our bench jumps up and rushes the field. We've won. Wait a minute, no. They, my teammates, have won the game. I didn't win anything.

Everybody goes nuts. I get up and join the others, just to shake the losing players' hands. Then I head back to the bench while all my teammates whoop and holler and congratulate one another.

The plan is for everyone to go to Jake's Place for burgers after the game, but I can't face the fun. I've got no business there. In fact, I was about a gnat's eyelash away from losing the game for everyone. Lo-Tone walks over and sticks his hand out. "A well-called game, Mr. Banks," he says in his phony British accent.

I just shake my head. "Are you trying to be funny?"

Lo-Tone looks more hurt than I've ever seen him, and thanks to my idiotic behavior, I've seen him look hurt quite a few times recently. He takes his hand away.

Dad, John-Two, Grandpa Will, and Mama Ev wait behind the fence with the other families. As soon as I reach them, Mama Ev throws her arms around me. "The championship! We're so proud of you boys."

"Thanks," I say. I'm glad no one asks me about the

substitution, but I'm sure they have a good idea why it happened.

"Clay," Lo-Tone yells from the infield. "Don't head over to Jake's without me."

"I'm not going," I yell back.

"Not going?" Mama Ev says. "What's the matter, child?"

"I don't feel like going."

"Don't you feel well?' She moves in to put her hand to my forehead.

I shrug her off. "No, I'm fine."

"Well, then you get your behind over to that party and be cordial," my dad says. "I didn't raise a spoiled brat who pouts when things don't go just his way."

"Yes, sir."

I must look pretty miserable because my dad softens. "Mistakes happen, son. Put it behind you and enjoy your victory. We'll see you later." He rubs my hair. I get hugs from Grandpa Will and Mama Ev, and a sock on the arm from John-Two.

I go join my teammates. "Hey, 'Tone, I'm sorry."

"No sweat, buddy," he says.

"It's just that—"

"You don't have to say anything." He lifts his chin in the direction of the bleachers. "Della's been standing over there sneaking peeks at you since the game ended. When are you gonna go talk to her?"

"I don't think I will."

"No?"

"No."

"You mean you're not going to invite her to Jake's?"

"No."

"Well, if you're not, you won't mind if I do?"

"Knock yourself out."

Lo-Tone trots over to Della. I see him talking to her. She shakes her head and glances over at me. Lo-Tone, I know, is turning on the Lo-Tone charm. She shrugs and nods, and the two of them start toward me. I wish Lo-Tone would mind his own business.

We walk to Jake's Place in a big group, so it's not overly obvious that I'm avoiding Della. The team bursts through the door in a riot of laughter, jokes, and roughhousing, and in two seconds every booth is filled. Jake's ready for us. He's got Cokes lined up in neat rows on the counter, a sign that reads "Congratulations, St. Paul's Trumpets—20–4," hanging on the wall, and hamburgers sizzling on the grill.

A number of my teammates have invited their sisters and girlfriends. I hang back and wait for Della and Lo-Tone to find seats, so I can sit somewhere else. Then Adelaide Crosbie saves me.

"Here, Clay!" she cries out. "Sit over here!"

I saunter over. Adelaide is a ninth grader, soon to be in tenth. She grew up two streets over from me. Her brother Leon is our left-fielder. She used to trick me into eating mud pies when we were little.

And she's still interested in food. "Are you gonna finish those fries?" she asks. "Are you done with your

burger? Do you think we can have seconds on Coke?"
She keeps my attention occupied by talking constantly,
about her cat, her unmanageable hair, her boyfriend,
Reginald, who'll be a senior—"Did you hear? A
senior!"—this year. It's fine with me because I don't have
to talk *or* think. Della has her back to me, so I can keep
an eye on her without her knowing about it. After what I
estimate is a polite amount of time, I mutter something
to Adelaide and Leon about getting home to do
something for some member of my family, say my good-
byes, and slip out while Della is in the bathroom.

I walk home alone and go straight up to my
bedroom. My family knows better than to bother me
now. And except for their "good nights," they don't try to
talk with me. Earlier this week I felt like I knew what I
believed, I felt so sure of myself; so I've got to ask now,
Why am I so miserable?

Here's a possibility: I've been denied one thing I
want, been told I have to wait until I grow up enough to
make my own decisions. I don't want to wait, so I've
turned into this monster. I almost lost the game with my
big head, trying to prove I was ready, and I seem to be
doing all I can to turn away my best friend. And Della,
the most beautiful girl on the planet, the girl I've been
pining away for, for five years, turns out to be from a
family that's made a religion out of turning the other
cheek.

As I lie in bed staring at the ceiling, I think about
something my Dad always has told me: Every action can

be judged by its consequence. If that's the case, my actions have been worse than I ever imagined they could be. How could things be going so wrong when all I've been doing is trying to do right?

Chapter 9

Sunday starts out a scorcher. Eight-thirty in the morning on the way to church and it's already 86° in the shade. We all move really slowly, but we're still damp with sweat by the time we get to St. Paul's.

You can barely hear Reverend Johnson over the sound of the prayer books flapping as everybody fans themselves trying to keep cool.

"I'll make the sermon brief today, brothers and sisters, for I'm sure the Lord never intended his faithful to melt into their shoes just so his long-winded spokesmen could pontificate to their hearts' content."

"Amen!" says old, hard-of-hearing Otis Kimbro from the last pew. Everyone laughs.

"I'll let Mrs. Octavia Carter read the announcements, and then we can sing one more hymn and then all go home to our electric fans and our porch swings." He pauses. No one says anything. "Do we have to let Mr. Kimbro speak for all of us? How does that sound?"

"Amen!" calls out the congregation.

"That's what I thought you'd say," he says. Then he turns. "Mrs. Carter?"

Mrs. Carter steps up to the lectern. First, she announces that the bake sale was a success, enriching the church's coffers by $63.75. Then, she calls on the baseball team to stand up and be congratulated for the championship victory. "Last, but certainly not least," she says. "You still have a week to get in your reservations for our trip to the March on Washington. So far, we have fourteen people signed up. We'd really like to fill a whole bus, brothers and sisters, so join us if you can. Remember, it's twenty dollars, and that includes transportation and meals.

"We're also calling for volunteers to help this week to encourage people in the community to join us. We need people to collect donations so that some of our congregation who could not otherwise afford to attend may make the trip. We also need help making placards and signs to carry during the march. If you'd like to help out with any of these activities, please speak with me after the service."

I've been preoccupied during most of the service, mostly staring at my big, shiny, black size 11 dress shoes and wondering when the rest of my body was going to catch up with my feet. But when Mrs. Carter started to speak about volunteers, I perked up. Dad might be able to forbid me to go to the march, but surely he couldn't object to my helping out in Wilson Park.

As the people file out after the service, I hang around the front walk waiting for Mrs. Carter to appear. I'm relieved to see that Dad is deep in conversation with Ruth and Earl Graves, our neighbors across the alley. Pretty soon, I see Mrs. Carter's butter-yellow hat making its way through the crowd. "Mrs. Carter." I call out.

"Clayton!" she cries in her summer breeze voice, and smothers me in a firm, lavender-scented embrace. "It has been so long since we've said hello. You're growing into such a busy young man."

"Not that busy, Mrs. Carter. That's what I want to talk to you about. I'd like to help out with the Washington trip."

"Oh, that's just wonderful, Clayton, wonderful. We have a lot to do and not much time. Why don't you come over tomorrow morning and we can get you to work on something?"

"That sounds fine."

And with another hug that pushes her hat askew, she bustles away. I go find my family, and on the walk home I feel better than I have since this whole march idea began.

When I get to Mrs. Carter's, I'm amazed to see her

in tennis shoes, blue jeans, and a denim work shirt, with a multicolored flowered scarf tied around her head.

"Right on time, Clayton," she says. "I hope you're ready to work. There's a lot to do."

I'm equally amazed to see old Mr. Kimbro there with a paint brush in his hand.

"Hello, Clayton," he shouts.

"Hello, Mr. Kimbro," I shout back.

"I'll bet you didn't know Mr. Kimbro was a sign painter back during the Depression,'" Mrs. Carter says. "The Lord has blessed us with Mr. Kimbro's talents for our trip." Mr. Kimbro smiles and looks a little sheepish.

"You can help us paint signs today, Clayton. Or you can get on the phone and ask for donations. Or you can go out and put up these posters and ask people to sign up."

"I've never been too steady with a paint brush, Mrs. Carter," I say. "Why don't I go out and hang posters."

"That's fine," she says. "And I'm dressed for painting, not meeting the public, anyway."

Mrs. Carter hands me a big stack of posters, a staple gun, and a roll of packing tape, and I hit the streets. My goal is to blanket Wilson Park from top to bottom with these signs. I reach my first telephone pole, staple up a sign, and step back to admire my work. OK, it's a little crooked, but the message will get across:

Make Your Voices Heard
Join the March on Washington for Jobs and Freedom
August 28, 1963
Buses depart from St. Paul's A.M.E. Church
919 Fletcher Ave., Middlefield
Tuesday, August 27, 1963
9:00 A.M.
$20.00 includes transportation and meals
For reservations or more information call
Rev. Charles Johnson or Mrs. Octavia Carter
KLemper 5-2750

I work my way up and down the streets of the Wilson Park business district. It's no sweat stapling posters onto telephone poles, trees, construction sites, and boarded up windows, but I'm not sure what to expect when I step into the first business to ask for permission to hang a sign in the window. I stand before the door of the Gentlemen's Barber Shop on 12th Street and take a deep breath. I'm pretty sure I can't take a rejection like the one I got from Dad, but I have a job to do, so I throw back my shoulders and walk in.

"Good morning," says the barber, eyeballing my stack of signs. "Something tells me you're not here for a haircut."

"No, not today," I say. "I'm putting up signs announcing a trip to Washington, D.C., for the March for Jobs and Freedom. The trip is sponsored by St. Paul's

A.M.E., and we'd really like to get as many people as we can to come along. Would it be OK if I put a sign in your window?"

"It sure would, young man. You put it right on the door, where everyone can see it. In fact, you put one facing out and one facing in, so my customers can read it while they're sitting in the chair."

Back out on the street I'm relieved and overjoyed. That was easy! I go into the dry cleaners and the drug store; they're happy to display a poster. At our two taverns, I'm offered a Coke, but I can't stop, and I'm a Nehi man, anyway. At Sophisticated Ladies dress shop, Triangle Texaco, Archie's Rib Joint, Shelby's Ice Cream Scoopers, and Plaxico Hardware, I'm treated like a visiting dignitary. Everyone is glad to have the signs up. The only ones who say no are the people at the bank. They have a "no signs" policy but they seem very sorry about it, and some of them write down the information for themselves.

Jake's Place is next. I know I'll have no problem there, and I'm in the mood for a cold Nehi. I've been to dozens of stores, walked dozens of blocks, and talked to dozens of people, and I'm thirsty.

"Good afternoon, Clayton," Jake says. "What brings you here? Grape Nehi?"

"Well, yes, that would be good. But I'm also spreading the word about the March on Washington, telling people about the trip sponsored by St. Paul's."

"No foolin'?"

"Really," I say.

"Well, I've read about the march in the paper," says Jake, " and I've been thinking about how much I'd like to go."

"Well, why don't you? It only costs twenty dollars, and that includes transportation and meals."

"Oh, it's not the money, Clay," says Jake. "I have no one who could run the diner and I can't close it."

"What about Nadine?" I say, thinking about the waitress who has worked with Jake for as long as I've been alive, it seems.

"Oh, she could run the place, for sure, but have you ever tasted Nadine's cooking? It could starve a buzzard."

"I heard that!" Nadine calls from the back room.

"Nadine, you know this diner would cease to exist without you." Jake calls out.

"You know that's right," she calls back.

"But her cooking!" Jake pinches his nose.

I laugh. "Well, I can't go either."

"Why not?"

"My dad thinks only troublemakers march for causes."

"Oh, I'm sorry to hear that, son. But I'm sure your daddy has good reasons for feeling the way he does."

"Good for *him*," I say.

Jake raises his eyebrows. "You're old much longer than you're young, Clayton. You'll have plenty of time to make your own decisions."

"That's what Dad says."

"Your daddy's a smart man, Clayton. You may not agree with him now, but that doesn't mean there ain't some wisdom in his decisions."

In my head I know Jake's right, but my stomach just won't let me swallow it. "Being fourteen stinks," I say, with my chin in my hands.

Jake looks at me in astonishment for half a second, then he throws his head back and opens his mouth wide in a huge, booming laugh. When he finally calms down, he says, "You should try being fifty-nine!"

"At least you can do what you want," I say.

He laughs again. "You think your daddy's strict? You think your daddy keeps you from doing what you want to do? Take a look around you. This restaurant is *my* strict daddy." He reaches under the counter, brings up a steel box, and opens the lid. "See these bills? Each of these is one very strict daddy." He snaps the lid shut and puts the box back behind the counter. "Every customer who walks in here is a strict daddy. Because if they're hungry for a hamburger and they see a cold grill and a locked door with a 'Gone fishin'' sign—or even one that says 'Gone marchin' for freedom and jobs'—how many times you think they gonna come back? Your daddy's just preparing you for the army of strict daddies that'll be running your life when you grow up."

I sip my Nehi. "I guess everything is just a little too depressing."

"Not at all," says Jake. "I wouldn't have it any other way. This place is my home, my livelihood, the place where all my friends gather. It takes a lot, sure. But it

104

gives back far more."

I nod my head.

"And I bet you could say much the same about your daddy."

I finish my Nehi and tape up a sign in Jake's window. "Well, I have a few more signs to put up. And then I'll be heading back to Mrs. Carter's," I say.

"You'll be fine," Jake says.

"I know."

When I get back to Mrs. Carter's, I find her and Mr. Kimbro, now joined by a few more ladies of the church, hard at work painting signs. Mr. Carter, home from his job at the plant, is on the phone calling for donations. I still have a couple of hours before I need to go home and get ready for dinner, so I help out by rinsing brushes, stacking signs to dry, carrying paint cans, and stapling wooden handles to the signs.

As I work, I think about what Jake said to me. I figure he was really talking about commitment and responsibility, hard things that bring good rewards; and an idea slowly starts to form.

On the way home from Mrs. Carter's, I stop by Mama Ev's.

"Well, how was your first day of volunteering?" she asks, sitting me down at her kitchen table and pouring me a glass of iced tea.

"Really good," I say. "I hung signs all over town. Everybody I talked to was really nice."

"I know. I saw one of your signs at the drugstore," she says.

"I also talked to Jake," I say, and pause.

"Mmmm?"

"He really wants to go to the march, but he can't leave the diner. I'm thinking that maybe I could offer to cook for him there for two days, so he can go. I've learned a lot about cooking since Mom—I mean, since Dad and I have been doing the cooking—"

"It's all right, Junebug."

"Anyway, I think it would be a nice thing to do, for Jake. So he can go to the march and doesn't have to worry."

"You know, it *would* be a fine thing to do for Jake. And you know what? I think it's such a fine idea that I'll offer to help you over there, while you're helping Jake. How does that sound?"

"You would do that?" I cried. "Really?"

"I think it would be fun," says Mama Ev, "and I've always kind of wanted to try out my cooking on a larger audience."

"Mama Ev, you're the greatest. I'll ask him about it tomorrow, then," I say.

The next morning, Mrs. Carter puts me to work on the phone. This is not quite as easy as stapling up signs. I have to be polite and personable, and think of as many different ways to convince a person to give money as there are reasons *not* to. Mrs. Carter gives me some pointers.

"Start out with a friendly greeting, identify yourself, and then tell them what we're doing—going to the march and showing our support for the cause of civil rights," she instructs me. "Ask if they can come along. If they say no, then inquire whether they can help out someone who would like to go but who can't afford the bus fare. If they say no to that too, then get them talking by asking a question," she says. "But not any old yes-or-no question. Try to get them to think, just a bit. 'What do you think the government in Washington is doing to help you, Mrs. Somebody?' or 'What is one of the ways you stand up for your rights, Mr. Somebody?' Then ask for money again. If they are firm about saying no, then tell them if they change their mind, they can call the church, and give them the number. Use good grammar and try not to say 'um' too much. Got all that?"

"I'll try," I say. It's a lot to remember, and the first few calls don't go so well. I stumble and forget some important points to make and say "um" a lot. But after a while it starts to get easier. And by the afternoon, it's almost fun. Sure, there are people who just don't want to talk at all. And one person even hangs up on me. But most people are polite, and quite a few have some very interesting things to say about the march, about Dr. King, and about their feelings about equality. Some even tell me about their experiences. One man tells me that he moved up to St. Louis with his family in 1921, after a race riot destroyed his entire neighborhood, Greenwood, the black section of Tulsa, Oklahoma.

I make calls all day until my ear feels like a limp piece of lettuce. But I collect pledges for $42, and Mrs. Carter is very happy with me. "We'll fill up that bus yet!" she calls out as I head down the walk. Before I go home, I have to go to Jake's Place to tell him about my idea. If he goes for it, that'll be one more person on the bus.

I walk in, make a beeline for the counter, sit down, and order a Nehi. "How's life in the salt mines?" Jake asks.

"Just fine, Jake, my man," I say. "But I think you look like you need a little break. How would you like it if my grandma and I do the cooking while Nadine runs the place, so you can go to the march?"

"Heh, heh, heh, you're kidding, right?" he asks.

"No, Jake. I'm serious. You and I both *want* to go. I'm not allowed to go. But you *would* go if the diner could stay open, and Mama Ev and I will keep it open for you. What do you think?"

Jake reflects on it a moment. His face is serious, and I'm afraid that he's going to say no, or, worse yet, that he's offended. But suddenly his face breaks wide open into one of those famous Jake Taplin-style grins, and he leans across the counter and grabs me by the shoulders. "Why, yes!" he says. "Yes, indeed!" Then he gets serious again. "You've talked this over with your grandma? It's OK with her?"

"Yes," I say. "She's excited about it."

"Well, dip me in molasses and call me sweet!" Jake says. "If you two don't mind flipping burgers and frying

108

potatoes for two days, you're on." He puts out his hand for a shake.

I shake.

"Hey," he calls over my shoulder. "Do you hear what your friend has offered to do for me?"

Who could he be talking to? I turn around. There, in the back booth, are Lo-Tone and Della. My jaw drops and my throat swallows involuntarily. Lo-Tone and Della don't look any more comfortable.

"Hey, Clay," Lo-Tone says. "No, Jake. I didn't hear. What's Clay doing for you?"

I don't hear Jake's reply. I'm looking at Della, who is looking down at a chocolate soda in front of her. For some reason, I'm noticing how her lashes form perfect small black arcs as they lie under her eyes, and how her perfect pink fingernails are lined up, left finger, right finger, on the soda glass, which she's gripping with both hands.

"—on the bus," Jake is saying.

I look from Jake to Lo-Tone, and they're both looking at me. "Yeah, it should be a fun trip," I say. Whether that had anything to do with what they were talking about, I don't wait to find out. "Well, I better get going," I say. "I don't want to be late for dinner." I get up casually. "I'll talk to you tomorrow, Jake. See ya later, Lo-Tone. Bye Della."

"Bye, Clay," they all say.

I stroll out of Jake's and as soon as I get out of sight, I start to run. I run all the way home and when I get there

I collapse on the front porch. I tell myself, *It's better this way.* But if it's really better, why does it feel so awful?

The rest of the week, I'm a volunteering fool. I'm at Mrs. Carter's at eight o'clock in the morning, painting signs. I'm on the phone asking for money. I'm covering every telephone pole in town with posters, and when they fall down or get torn off, I replace them. I'm visiting the people who've made pledges, to collect the money they've promised. I'm even doing Mrs. Carter's grocery shopping. I don't stop. Because if I stop, I'll start to think, and if I think, I'm starting to learn, I'll get in trouble.

Then every night after dinner, Mama Ev and I go over to Jake's Place to learn the ropes. Jake makes us swear a solemn oath to keep his special recipes—for chili, for fried chicken, for barbecue sauce, for baked beans, and for sweet potato pie—a secret. He shows us how to grill the hamburgers so the meat is lacy and crispy around the edges and juicy in the middle. By the end of the week, Jake is convinced no one will even know he's gone.

Chapter 10

By the time Saturday arrives, Mrs. Carter's team has collected $211 and signed up 48 more people, enough to almost fill two buses. We've painted enough signs to wallpaper Sportsman's Park. At the end of the day, Mr. Carter shows up with pizzas and Cokes, and we all relax and bask in our accomplishments—Mr. and Mrs. Carter, Mr. Kimbro, the church ladies, and me.

Walking home afterward, I'm almost sad that it's all over. I've been so busy all week I haven't had time to feel bad about not going. Now that the feeling is coming back, I have to tell myself to think about something else.

John-Two is getting ready to go to Chicago for his meeting with the SNCC guys. He hasn't told Dad what the agenda of the meeting is, and I don't blame him. The three Banks men have all been getting along this week by avoiding controversial topics—that is, one another.

When I get home, Dad is in his chair, a magazine in his lap, snoozing. John-Two is upstairs in his room packing his suitcase.

"You're home early tonight," he says.

"Tomorrow's the last day to sign up for the trip, so we're basically all done," I say.

"I sometimes wish I could say that."

"You know what I mean."

"I'm just being dramatic," he says. He gets a stack of shirts from the closet and begins taking them off their hangers and folding them neatly. "I tried to bring up the march with Dad, you know, put in a good word for you, but he was having none of it."

"Why's he so nuts about it?"

"I've been trying to figure that one out myself," says John-Two. "The best I can come up with is that he's just scared."

"Scared?"

"Yeah. Scared for us, scared of a world that's changing faster than he is." John-Two sits down on the bed. "Dad has done pretty well in the world that he understands. And it's the only world he can teach us about. I think he believes that if he can keep us in his world, everything will be all right for us."

"Gosh, you make me feel bad for getting mad at him."

John-Two laughs. "Mad's OK, little brother, as long as you don't stop talkin'."

Before I go to bed, I go back downstairs to take a

peek at my dad. He's sound asleep, with his arm hanging down off the armrest and his reading glasses dangling from his fingers. I tiptoe close to him and lift the magazine from his chest—it's *The Journal of the American Dental Association*—and put it on the end table. I take the glasses out of his hand and put them on top of the magazine.

On Sunday I'm back in church. Lo-Tone and I are ushers, as usual. As I'm walking up the church steps with my family, Lo-Tone takes me aside and says, "Clay, buddy, let me explain—"

"You don't have to," I say.

"But I do."

"Believe me. You don't."

Lo-Tone grabs me by the sleeve. "If I don't have to explain, then why haven't I talked to you in practically two weeks? When was the last time we didn't hardly speak in two weeks? Can't remember, can you? 'Cause it was never."

I just shake my head. It's something I'd rather not deal with right now. "We haven't stopped bein' friends, Lo-Tone."

"Then why have you been lyin' to me?"

"I don't know what you're talking about."

"You've been telling me in all kinds of ways that you don't care anything for Della Tillborn, so I think, 'OK, I can take her for a soda.' Then you show up at Jake's and when you see us there, your face goes south like you're lookin' at a car wreck."

"I just have a lot on my mind, that's all."

"Well, I don't know what's going on with you and Della but every time I see her, it's 'Clay this' and 'Clay that.' And after you left Jake's, she got all jittery and had to go home *right then*."

"Well, I don't know what to tell you," I say. "I'm sorry if I've made you feel weird. Why don't we get together for some whiffleball this afternoon?"

Lo-Tone smiles. "Yeah, that sounds good."

We settle down in the pew, and the rhythm of the service and the peacefulness of the hymns soothes me. After a while, the service is nearing its end, and Reverend Johnson says, "I'd like to thank and congratulate Mrs. Carter for organizing the trip to the march. Because of her efforts, we have, as of this minute, sixty-one people going to Washington, D.C. to represent St. Paul's. And Mrs. Carter tells me that one of our young congregants deserves special recognition for his tireless work all week to make this mission the success it has been. Clayton Banks, could you please stand up and be recognized?"

I can't believe my ears. Is the pastor telling me to stand up, all by myself?

"Clayton?"

I guess he is. I stand up. The congregation applauds. My dad looks as surprised as I feel. People sitting near him touch him on the shoulder and nod their approval.

Reverend Johnson continues. "Although Clayton won't be with us on the trip, he'll truly be with us in

Washington in spirit. Thank you, Clayton."

I glance over at John-Two, who shrugs his shoulders.

After the service, Dad, John-Two, Grandpa Will, Mama Ev, and I walk home. Mama Ev, as usual, bubbles over with enthusiastic praise for my success. Grandpa and John-Two compliment me as well. Only my dad is silent. I've gotten used to the fact that we just don't agree on this matter, but it still hurts a little that he won't even give me credit for doing a good job.

Grandpa Will and Mama Ev say good-bye when we reach their house, and the rest of us continue home. John-Two and I start upstairs to change clothes.

"Clayton," Dad says, "I want to talk with you a minute."

What could this be? I follow him into the kitchen and we both sit down.

"I was proud of you today at church," he says.

"Thank you."

"I didn't realize how hard you were working all week." His hands, clean and well manicured as always, lie half cupped on the kitchen table. We both stare at them. "I wasn't paying any attention to what you've been doing, and I'm sorry for that."

This is really hard for my dad, and I'm squirming in the kitchen chair too.

"Dad, it's OK. I was just doing what I felt like doing."

"Son, you did good, and you did it well. You made a lot of people happy this week."

"Dad, it's *OK*." It's funny how listening to

115

compliments from your own dad can be just as hard as listening to scolding. I kind of wish he'd stop, actually.

But then he delivers the shocker.

"I want you to go to the march," he says.

"You *want* me to go?"

"Well, I mean, if you still want to," he says. "Of course, it's your call."

"Yes," I say hesitantly. "I still want to."

"Well . . . good. Then you'd better get over to the church and make your reservation."

"But Dad, I can't go."

He looks at me in disbelief.

"I'm minding Jake's Place with Mama Ev, remember?"

"I had forgotten." Dad thinks for a moment. "Do you think Jake would accept a substitute?"

"I suppose."

"I'm not such a bad cook," Dad says. "I could reschedule a couple of appointments and be your stand-in."

Now I am excited. "You'd do that?"

"Yes."

I let out a whoop and throw my arms around my Dad.

"OK, OK, son," he says, patting my shoulder. "Now get going."

Sunday dinner is one of the best we've had in a long time. Everybody is so excited that no one can get a word in edgewise. When Grandpa Will hears that Dad's going to fill in for me at Jake's, he volunteers himself. "What else has an old retired geezer got to do? You take care of Wilson Park's teeth, like you're paid to do, and I'll cook at Jake's." Everybody laughs at that.

Part of the reason we're all extra happy at dinner is that we're also sad. It's John-Two's last dinner with us before he heads to Chicago for his SNCC meeting and then back to school. While we wash dishes after dinner, John-Two says to me, "You'll make a heck of an activist."

"No," I say. "I'm not brave like you. I don't even know what I believe in."

"I've watched you all this week, little brother. You're an activist. You may not know what you believe in, but it doesn't really matter. You can act. And even more important, you have a talent for getting people on your side just by doing what you feel like doing. And your heart's in the right place. That's the best kind of activism."

When we put him on the bus later and wave good-bye, it's the first time I don't feel he's leaving me behind. I have somewhere to go now too.

Chapter 11

Mama Ev and I go to Jake's Monday morning, as planned. We're pretty well trained by now, but we go just because it's fun. Today we have something important to discuss, and Grandpa Will joins us.

"The chefs have arrived!" says Jake as we walk in. "Hello, Mr. Maxwell. What a pleasant surprise!"

"Jake," I say. I can't even wait for us to get settled in. "I have an offer to make."

"If it's as good as the last one, I'm all ears," says Jake.

"How would you like two experienced cooks to run the diner when you're gone, plus one big fan to listen to your baseball stories all the way to Washington, D.C.?"

"Come again?"

"What Clayton is trying to say—and taking the long route about it," Mama Ev says, "is that his daddy has given him permission to attend the march and my husband, a formidable cook in his own right, has volunteered to take Clay's place here at the diner while you're gone."

"You're willing to do that for me?" Jake asks Grandpa Will.

"Yes, for you, and for Clay."

"Well, that's fine. That's just fine," Jake says.

"I'm a fast learner," Grandpa Will says.

"And he already makes the best pancakes in Missouri," I say.

"All right, then!" says Jake. "Let's get to gettin'."

So Mama Ev and I cut potatoes, slap hamburger patties, chop onions, slice tomatoes, roll pastry, and generally have a great time getting ready for the lunch crowd, while Grandpa Will and Jake take care of the folks in for breakfast. "You're right," Jake says. "These pancakes of your grandpa's are something special."

"Jake, we're getting low on flour here," Grandpa Will says.

"I'll get it," says Mama Ev. "I have to visit the ladies' anyway."

Mama Ev goes to the back room and we all continue our chores. It's pretty busy, but eventually Grandpa Will says, "Where has that woman gotten to?"

"Oh, she's probably back there reading labels," I say.

"I'll go fetch her," Grandpa Will says. He disappears into the back room and a second later we hear him cry, "Ev! Ev! Jake, Clay, come quick!"

We run to the back room. Mama Ev lies unconscious on the floor with her arm wrapped around a 20-pound sack of flour.

"I just found her like this," Grandpa Will says. He pats her cheeks, getting flour on them, soft white hand prints on her smooth brown cheeks. I think it's a strange thing for me to notice. "Ev? Ev? Can you hear me?" Grandpa Will calls loudly. "Wake up!"

Jake runs to call an ambulance. Grandpa Will starts to give Mama Ev mouth-to-mouth resuscitation. It's only a few minutes before the ambulance arrives, but it seems like forever. Grandpa Will works on Mama Ev while I stand there, praying for her and also praying that it's not my fault. *I got her into this,* I tell myself. Looking at the sack of flour, now pushed out of the way by Grandpa Will, I can't help but think I should have known that this kind of work was too hard for her.

Grandpa Will rides with Mama Ev in the ambulance, and Jake gives me a ride to the hospital in his truck. "I'll call your daddy for you," he says as he drops me off.

It doesn't take the doctors long to discover that Mama Ev has had a stroke. One of the emergency room doctors, a tall man with thinning hair, comes to talk with us.

"We're not sure how long she was lying there," he tells us. "So we don't know how severe the damage to the brain is. You should be prepared for her not making it through the night. But if she does, she has a good chance of recovery."

Grandpa Will seems to only hear the words "good chance of recovery." He stays by her side all day and all night, holding her hand and encouraging her in a cheerful voice: "Honey, the doctors say you're going to be just fine. You've got many more years left. Just hold on, honey. We'll get through this." It doesn't seem to matter to him that she is unconscious.

Dad and I go home. Grandpa Will seems to want to be alone with Mama Ev. Later that evening, Daddy reaches John-Two in Chicago and tells him what has happened. "Just stay in touch," I hear him say before hanging up. When Dad gets off the phone, he tells me that John-Two asked him if he should come home.

"How could he ask that question?" I say. "Of course he should be here. How selfish could a person be? What could be more important than being with the family right now?"

"I told him there was nothing he could do here," Dad says stoically.

"You should've made him come home."

"It's his call to make."

I understand, but the words are too heavy, and I don't respond.

Much to the doctors' surprise and delight, Grandpa Will was right: Mama Ev has held on. By Wednesday she's breathing on her own. Her room is filling up with flowers and cards. Friends and relatives from all over the country have been calling to see how she's doing. I knew we loved her, but I'm just realizing how much she means to other people.

Mama Ev's stroke has taken out her right side, so she can't do much of anything. Her speech is slurred, but I can understand her, mostly. She has a hard time finding the right words to use. It's tough for her, and for Grandpa Will. I think they need me to be here, to help them. So Washington is out. I've decided not to go. I haven't told anybody, but I think it's the right thing to do.

By Saturday, she's doing well enough for a real visit. The four of us talk for a while, or rather, Grandpa Will, Dad, and I talk, and Mama Ev seems happy just to listen. When the phone rings, she says, "Answer the cup." I think she's embarrassed about her speech problems.

Dad and Grandpa Will leave the room to get sodas and stretch their legs.

Mama Ev takes a deep breath and looks out the window for a minute. She studies a robin that has landed on the ledge. The robin flies away, and Mama Ev turns her attention back to me.

"Junebug," Mama Ev says softly, and motions me to her bed. I walk over to her.

"Junebug, you still . . . you still . . . ?" She's frustrated. "Washington. You still?"

I'm surprised. Why is she asking? Does she think I'm going to leave her?

"No, Mama Ev," I say, taking her hand in mine. "I'll be here. I'm not going anywhere."

She shakes her head to the side, and moves her hand out of mine.

"No. No." she blurts.

"What?"

"Go. Go. Promise you go."

I can't promise her something I know I can't do. But she keeps insisting.

"Go. Go. Promise you go. Promise."

Just then, Dad and Grandpa Will come in.

"What's going on?" Dad asks. "Is Ev all right?"

I'm shaking. I think I've made her sick.

"I told her that I wasn't going to Washington, and she's having a fit. What did I do wrong? I thought she'd be happy."

Grandpa Will and Dad calm her down while I stand off to the side, begging God to keep her from getting worse. "I'll do what you want me to do, God," I say silently. "I just don't want her to get worse. What must I do?"

"Clayton," Grandpa Will says. "Son, I can't tell you what to do. She wants you to go because she knows how important this is to you."

"But, I don't want to leave her while she's sick," I say, cutting him off.

"Clayton, your grandmother is not alone. We're family. She'll be here when you come back, wanting to hear all the details."

I look at Dad. "What do you think?"

Dad, stoic as he's always been, says, "It's your call."

Dad says he's going to stay at the hospital, and I decide to go home. It's only a two-mile walk back to the house. There's nothing I can do at the hospital anyway, and Grandma Ev has drifted off to sleep.

I walk down to the front of the hospital, and there's Lo-Tone waiting for me.

"How's Mama Ev?" Lo-Tone asks. "She all right?"

Mama Ev has always looked at Lo-Tone as a third grandchild. "Well, he eats like a third grandchild," she always jokes.

"She's better. She's better," I say, looking at my shoes.

It seems like an eternity, just standing there. I don't know what to say, but I have to start somewhere.

"Lo-Tone," I start, looking not at him, but at the trees to the left of him. "I'm sorry. I've been a real jerk, a complete knucklehead loser."

I turn my eyes back at him. Lo-Tone looks at me.

"Keep going, Clay. You're on a roll," Lo-Tone says.

I'm sort of in shock. But then I notice he's got a smile on his face. "Yep, you've been a real pain-in-the-behind lately, but I forgive you," he says. Then he punches me in the arm.

That's another of the many great qualities about Lo-Tone: He's got a good heart and an understanding soul. I may be one of the smartest kids in class, but Lo-Tone, on more than one occasion, has shown that he is one of the wisest and kindest.

We walk along the sidewalk, down streets that we've walked a thousand times. The branches of the tall elms and oaks that line Harrison, Van Buren, and Pershing streets are a cool green arch above our heads. We walk past the houses of people that I've known all my life: the Nelsons, Dr. and Mrs. Frazier, the Woodses, the Browns.

But I feel like I'm a million miles away. Should I stay? Should I go?

"What's up, brother?" Lo-Tone asks.

"Uh, well, I'm thinking about whether I should go to Washington or not."

Lo-Tone stops in his tracks.

"What?" he says. "This . . . What? Have you lost your cotton-pickin' mind? After all your work, and your dad agreein' to let you go? You have to go!"

"What about Mama Ev, Lo-Tone?" I retort.

"Did you talk to her about it?" Lo-Tone asks.

"Yeah."

"And I bet she told you to go," he says.

"Yes, but I don't know if she meant it. What's she going to say, 'No, don't go.' I can't see her telling me that."

"If she really wanted you to stay, she would've told you," Lo-Tone says. "She's always been a straight shooter."

We start walking again. After a couple of feet, he asks, "Clay, you still going to go, right? I mean, I'm counting on you. What's it going to be without you?"

I just smile. I'm pretty sure I have the answer, but I just want to see Lo-Tone squirm a bit.

"Yo, Clay, man, please, I don't want to be on that hot bus with all those old church people. Ya gotta go. You owe me. I've been carrying you since we were in kindergarten."

I just keep smiling.

"Oh, funny boy, you keep smilin'. But if you ain't on the bus to Washington, I'm going to make your freshman year a miserable experience."

I laugh out loud. Lo-Tone swats me in the back of the head.

"Lo-Tone, I took on my Dad. Do you think your love taps and idle threats are going to twist me one way or another?"

"Let me guess," Lo-Tone says. "It's your call to make."

And with that I tag him on the back.

"Last one to my house is a rotten egg!"

Chapter 12

When I leave for the church at 6:45 on Tuesday morning, I fully expect to be the first one there. But, wonder of wonders, when I arrive Lo-Tone is already there. Just like me, he's carrying an overnight bag and a paper sack, which I know is full of snacks for the trip.

"You're early for once," I say to him.

"I couldn't sleep, so I figured I'd be here to greet everybody," he says. "So—greetings!"

"I didn't sleep either, but I went with Dad and Grandpa Will over to Jake's to get them going. Jake's on his way."

"This is going to be some trip!" says Lo-Tone.

"Yeah," I say.

Lo-Tone opens his bag and peers in. "I've got apple juice, and 'Nilla Wafers . . . potato chips . . . hmmm . . . one, two, *three* Mars bars, and two bologna sandwiches."

"Sounds good," I say.

"And Della's coming," Lo-Tone says, with his face still in the bag.

"What?"

"Della's coming," he repeats in a tiny voice.

"That's great," I say sarcastically. "I thought it was you and me."

He puts the bag down. "It was—it is," he says. "I just found out myself day before yesterday. You know her auntie was supposed to go, but her cousin just had her baby early, and now Della's going in her auntie's place."

I glare at him.

"Surprise!" he says, sheepishly.

"Don't be a funny guy," I say. "I can tell you I'm not sitting with her for eighteen hours on the bus."

"What is going on with you two?" Lo-Tone demands. "This is getting stupid. You better tell me."

I figure I'm not going to be able to keep it a secret from him forever, so I tell him about the fishing trip.

"That's *it?*" he says, tagging me on the head.

"That's enough."

Lo-Tone looks at me like he's never seen me before.

"You've got some screwed-up ideas, Poindexter, but this one takes the cake."

"If you can't see how the way they acted was screwed up," I say, "then you're the screwed-up one."

"Well, maybe you should explain it to me." Lo-Tone is sarcastic, and I'm not used to that tone from him.

"First of all, this ranger at the gate is looking us up and

down, like he's *deciding* whether to let us in, and the Tillborns don't say a thing. They just sit there and answer his questions."

"Did the ranger insult them?"

"No."

"What did he ask, then?"

"He asked if we were fishing. How long we were staying, the whole third-degree."

"Was he rude?"

"No."

"Did he charge them more to get in?"

"No."

"Did he call Mr. Tillborn boy?"

"No."

"Then what were they supposed to do?"

"I don't know. But what about the kids with their dirt clod and their 'We don't eat no *coon* food.' "

"That's pretty bad."

"Yeah, it's bad!"

"What were the Tillborns supposed to do about it?"

"*Say* something! *Do* something!"

"Like what?"

"Tell them—tell them—I don't know *what*, exactly. Tell them they can't get away with that!" I'm angry again just thinking about it. "I mean, I tried to go after those punks, and the Tillborns acted mad at *me*, like *I* was doing something out of line."

"You don't get out much, do you?" Lo-Tone asks.

"I don't know what you mean."

"I mean, how often do you get out of Wilson Park?"

"Uhh—"

"Yeah. 'Uhh,' " Lo-Tone says mockingly. "Your daddy believes in keeping separate, the way things are. You don't know what it's like, how to deal with ignorant people like that because he keeps you away from them, mostly. The Tillborns go more places than you guys do. Maybe that's just the way they get along."

"If that's getting along—" I sputter. "*You* may go along to get along, but times are changing, and I can't back up that mentality."

"They had fun, didn't they? They did what they wanted to do on a Sunday afternoon, didn't they?"

I don't know how to respond to that, and Lo-Tone getting in the last word really ticks me off. But the buses have arrived, and other people are starting to gather, so it's a good time to end our discussion.

Jake walks up with a cup of coffee. "Hey, Clay, traveling buddy!" he booms. "Hey, Anthony." He shakes our hands.

"Should we climb on the bus, get a good seat in front?" Jake asks.

"Sure," I say.

"I'll wait out here," says Lo-Tone.

As Jake disappears into the bus, I lean over and hiss at Lo-Tone. "You ride on the other bus."

He shakes his head. "Whatever."

I never get tired of hearing Jake's stories of the old

Negro baseball leagues. These were the leagues, popular from the 1920s to the 1940s, for black players only. At that time, black players were not allowed to play on the Major League teams. But black players wanted to play— and they played brilliantly—and black fans wanted to watch, so the Negro American League, the Negro National League, the Negro Southern League, and others had their teams, their rivalries, their seasons, and their stars, just like the Major Leagues. Separate but equal.

I love repeating the team names—the Chicago American Giants, the Kansas City Monarchs, the Pittsburgh Crawfords—and the colorful names of the star players. There was Mule Suttles, Buck Leonard, Biz Mackey, Smokey Joe Williams, Rube Foster, Pee Wee Butts, Double Duty Radcliffe, Cool Papa Bell, and Cristobel Torrienti, not to mention the incomparable pitcher Satchel Paige and the legendary slugger Josh Gibson.

Jake and I shoot the breeze, about the Negro Leagues, Little League, running a diner, growing up in South Carolina in the early 1900s, being a high-school freshman, all kinds of stuff, for the first few hours as the rolling cornfields of Illinois and Indiana flash by like the frames in a movie. Then, all talked out, we mostly sit quietly, and I drink in the scenery as it unfolds outside the window: the green horse pastures and forested mountains of Kentucky, the rugged peaks and rushing streams of West Virginia. Sometimes the people in the bus sing hymns and spirituals to pass the time, or they share food and drink, tell jokes, or wonder aloud about what awaits us in D.C.

Eventually it begins to grow dark. We stop for a short bathroom break and we get a new bus driver and continue on our way. People quiet down and I slump in my seat to try to catch some Z's.

I must be successful because there seems to be a glow in the sky as Jake shakes me awake. "Look, Clay," he says.

We're crossing a river—I find out later it's the Potomac—and the water is like a silver ribbon in the dim, brand-new morning light.

"We're here," he says.

We're early enough that there are few other buses on the streets of the capital, and we roll into the bus parking area across from the White House with no problems or delays.

"So that's the White House," I say, pressing my nose against the window. "Wow!"

"Wow is right," says Jake.

The bus lurches to a halt, and we file out and then stand there, all of us, rubbing our eyes and wondering where we can go to freshen up.

"Clayton Banks!" I turn just in time to see Della barreling down on me like a line drive. Before I can duck, I get a sharp slap across the face.

"Ow!" I rub my cheek.

"I'd hit you with a board if I had one," she says. "So, you think my family is some kind of bunch of Uncle Toms, is that right?"

"Lo-Tone," I moan, looking around for the culprit.

"Oh, no. You're not blaming this on Lo-Tone," she says, her eyes smoldering with fury.

"I didn't say Uncle Toms."

"Well, that's what you meant! How dare you suggest that we let white people walk all over us! How dare you, when we invited you to spend the day with us and fed you *and taught you how to fish!*" as though that was the highest honor of all. "How dare you pass judgment on the way we handle ourselves!"

"I'm . . . I'm sorry. I didn't mean it like that," I say, but in my heart I know I did, and I feel ashamed.

She knows it too. "You most very well did, Clayton Banks, and I will appreciate it very much if you never speak to me again." She stomps off.

I just stand there, with my hand on my cheek.

"Ouch, that was ugly," Jake says.

"I don't want to talk about it."

"I hear ya," Jake says. "Let's go find the facilities."

We head off in the direction of the comfort stations near Constitution Avenue, walking in silence until Jake, out of the blue, asks me, "When I say 'Satchel Paige,' what comes to mind?"

"What brings that up?"

"Just answer the question."

"Gosh, Jake, that's obvious—a sports hero, one of the greatest pitchers who ever lived, Lo-Tone's number-one favorite ball player next to Bob Gibson, a pitcher who could outsmart any batter with his wily moves."

"Do you think of him as a clown?" Jake asks.

"No."

"A black who gave the rest of us blacks a bad image?"

"Huh?"

"Of course you don't. You know him the way history will remember him, for his talents and his baseball legacy. But back when he was pitching, he was known as much for his clowning and theatrics on the field as he was for his pitching." Jake chuckles, with a faraway look that tells me he has more memories than there is time to share them. "One time, Satchel gets a little feisty, I guess, feels unusually confident when the top of the other team's lineup is up. So he sends his entire infield to the bench— just tells 'em all to go sit down—while he faces the meanest sluggers on the team."

"So what happened?"

"He struck out the side, just like he planned."

"Cool."

"Sure," says Jake. "But not everybody appreciated that kind of grandstanding. Players who took the game more seriously resented his making the games into a joke and taking attention away from their solid skills. Black newspaper writers criticized him for portraying an unflattering image of blacks. They were afraid he'd set back the hopes of black players to someday make it into the Major Leagues."

"Did he?" I ask.

"Depends on how you look at it," Jake says. "As for me, I think Satchel was one smart cat, besides having an arm like a violin string. He knew how to take all the parts

of himself—not only the athlete, but also the clown, the
bragger, the strategist—to make himself into somebody
people wanted to pay to see. I don't think Jackie Robinson
would have been signed by the Brooklyn Dodgers in 1947
if it hadn't been for Satchel. Other people may not agree,
but it's my opinion."

The march is planned to begin about 11:30 at the
Washington Monument at the east end of the Mall. It will
proceed westward on either side of the reflecting pool
about three quarters of a mile to the Lincoln Memorial,
where a number of speeches will be delivered. Most of us
know that Martin Luther King's speech promises to be the
highlight of the day.

We grab our signs and make our way to the
Washington Monument at seven o'clock. Jake has changed
from his traveling clothes into his "marching threads," a
very snazzy double-breasted suit and a purple silk tie. I've
changed into a clean shirt, but it's pretty rumpled from
being in the bag all night.

Already there are a few hundred people at the
monument, and we make our way over there to await the
beginnings of the festivities. Jake and I stroll around to
drink in the sights before it gets too crowded to move.

"Check out the goon squad," Jake says, jerking his
chin in the direction of a grassy area near the Washington
Monument. About 50 scrawny, scowling white guys, with
their arms folded, stand there, just staring. They're
surrounded by almost as many police officers.

"Who are they?"

"Nazis," says Jake. "I read in the paper they were planning to show up."

"What are they doing here?"

"Registering their disagreement, I guess," Jake says dryly.

Suddenly there's a ruckus from the direction of the buses. A rowdy group of teenagers, led by a tall guy in a bright red shirt, approaches us.

The tall guy claps and sings, "Freedom, freedom, freedom, freedom. Goin' to take it to the President."

And his followers sing, "Yeah, man."

The tall guy sings, "Goin' to take it to the Capital."

And his followers sing, "Yeah, man."

"Goin' to take it to the press."

"Yeah, man."

"Goin' to see it on the news."

"Yeah, man."

"Goin' to shout it from the mountain top."

"Shout it!"

"Are you satisfied?"

"Satisfied!"

"Freedom."

"Freedom."

"Yeah, man."

"Yeah, man."

This is better than I could have imagined. As the morning progresses, more and more people gather. There are people there from all over the country, and the world.

We're in a sea of beautiful faces of every shade, most of them brown, but about every tenth one is white. There are old people, young people, nuns and priests, Muslims in head scarves, people in wheelchairs, some on crutches, pregnant women and babes in arms. All together, they are talking, singing, praying, laughing, shaking their signs. Some are rowdy and some are serene. Some are in their Sunday best. Others wear the uniforms of their work, or casual blue jeans. Some carry parasols for shade, while others tip their face toward the sky like sunflowers. But everyone, every single person there, walks with dignity and pride. In my mind, I compare these people—my people—to the Nazis, all ragged and surly and full of hate and out of place on their patch of grass, and it really hits me, all that we have to be proud of.

Then, at 11:20, the crowd starts to move. Without warning, and without instruction, it just decides, like it's one big organism, that it's time to march. We walk along, and it's mostly quiet. I can hear the shuffling of thousands of feet, and although we are shoulder to shoulder and the sun beats down on our heads, I feel cool and light, and suddenly I look over at Della and I understand what Lo-Tone, Jake, and even John-Two, without knowing it, have been trying to explain to me; that the Tillborns were taking a stand in their own way, by *knowing* they belonged and never letting somebody else's bigotry shake that belief. And they were so firm in their belief that it didn't even put a dent in their joy, not for one second.

I work my way over to where Lo-Tone and Della are

walking. "Della," I begin.

She looks at me with no expression at all.

"Della, I've been thinking. I know now I was wrong. And I know why I was wrong. And I hope you'll forgive me and be my friend."

She lowers her eyes, then raises them to mine. "There will be time for that, Clay. Now it's time to march."

That's going to have to be good enough, for now.

The speeches all run together in my mind. I remember John Lewis, the founder of SNCC, and the fire and anger in his words of peace. I remember the singing of "We Shall Overcome." But most of all, as usual, I'm thinking about myself, and hoping it's not too late to make changes.

Finally, it's announced that the next speaker is Dr. Martin Luther King, Jr., who has just been released from a Montgomery jail for peaceful demonstrations.

Dr. King takes the podium and begins to speak: You can hear a pin drop on cotton. The wind snaps the American flag, and a jet hums overhead. But other than that, there are no other sounds, except the affirmations of the crowd as they respond to the emotions that Dr. King so elegantly expresses.

"I am happy to join with you today in what will go down in history as the greatest demonstration for freedom in the history of our nation," he says.

"Go 'head. Go 'head," says the crowd.

"Five score years ago, a great American, in whose symbolic shadow we stand today, signed the Emancipation

Proclamation. This momentous decree came as a great beacon light of hope to millions of Negro slaves, who had been seared in the flames of withering injustice. It came as a joyous daybreak to end the long night of their captivity."

"Thank you, Lord."

"But one hundred years later, the Negro is still not free. One hundred years later, the life of the Negro is still sadly crippled by the manacles of segregation and the chains of discrimination."

"Tell the truth."

"One hundred years later the Negro lives on a lonely island of poverty in the midst of a vast ocean of material prosperity.

"One hundred years later the Negro is still languished in the corners of American society and finds himself an exile in his own land. . . .

"We have . . . come to this hallowed spot to remind America of the fierce urgency of now. . . . Now is the time to rise from the dark and desolate valley of segregation to the sunlit path of racial justice. Now is the time to lift our nation from the quicksands of racial injustice to the solid rock of brotherhood. Now is the time to make justice a reality for all of God's children." . . .

"Amen."

"There will be neither rest nor tranquility in America until the Negro is granted his citizenship rights. . . ."

"Tell the truth."

"We must forever conduct our struggle on the high plain of dignity and discipline. We must not allow our creative protest to degenerate into physical violence. Again and again, we must rise to the majestic heights of meeting physical force with soul force."

"Amen."

"The marvelous new militancy which has engulfed the Negro community must not lead us to a distrust of all white people, for many of our white brothers, as evidenced by their presence here today, have come to realize that their destiny is tied up with our destiny. . . .

"Let us not wallow in the valley of despair. I say to you today, my friends: so even though we face the difficulties of today and tomorrow, I still have a dream. It is a dream deeply rooted in the American dream.

"I have a dream that one day this nation will rise up and live out the true meaning of its creed—we hold these truths to be self-evident that all men are created equal."

"Thank you, Lord."

"I have a dream that one day on the red hills of Georgia the sons of former slaves and the sons of former slave owners will be able to sit together at the table of brotherhood.

"I have a dream that one day even the state of Mississippi, a state sweltering with the heat of injustice, sweltering with the heat of oppression, will be transformed into an oasis of freedom and justice.

"I have a dream that my four little children will one day live in a nation where they will not be judged by the color of their skin but by the content of their character."

"Go 'head. Go 'head."

"I have a dream today!

"I have a dream that one day, down in Alabama, with its vicious racists, with its governor having his lips dripping with the words of interposition and nullification; one day right there in Alabama little black boys and black girls will be able to join hands with little white boys and white girls as sisters and brothers."

"Amen!" cries the crowd.

"I have a dream today!

"I have a dream that one day every valley shall be exalted, every hill and mountain shall be made low, the rough places will be made plain and the crooked places will be made straight and the glory of the Lord shall be revealed and all flesh shall see it together."

"Praise God!"

"This is our hope. This is the faith that I will go back to the South with. With this faith we will be able to hew out of the mountain of despair a stone of hope.

"With this faith we will be able to transform the jangling discords of our nation into a beautiful symphony of brotherhood. With this faith we will be able to work together, to pray together, to struggle together, to go to jail together, to stand up for freedom together, knowing that we will one day be free. . . .

"And so let freedom ring from the prodigious hilltops of New Hampshire.

"Let freedom ring from the mighty mountains of New York.

"Let freedom ring from the heightening Alleghenies of

Pennsylvania.

"Let freedom ring from the snow-capped Rockies of Colorado.

"Let freedom ring from the curvaceous slopes of California.

"But not only that."

Dr. King pauses, and I hold my breath. "Tell the truth," mutters the crowd.

And he continues, "Let freedom ring from the Stone Mountain of Georgia.

"Let freedom ring from Lookout Mountain of Tennessee.

"Let freedom ring from every hill and molehill of Mississippi, from every mountainside, let freedom ring!

"And when this happens, when we allow freedom to ring, when we let it ring from every village and every hamlet, from every state and every city, we will be able to speed up that day when all of God's children, black men and white men, Jews and Gentiles, Protestants and Catholics, will be able to join hands and sing in the words of the old Negro spiritual, 'Free at last, free at last. Thank God Almighty, we are free at last!' "

And the roar that arises from the crowd at the end of Dr. King's speech is like nothing I've ever heard, or, I will come to learn, like anything I will ever hear again. It's a roar of joy, of longing, of pride and sadness, a roar that wraps itself around every wound, every scar, every fear in the heart of every man, woman, and child in that crowd, and flings it upward, to heaven, in one full-throated, beseeching bellow of hope.

And then, remarkably, it's over. There's nothing much to say to add to what we've just shared, and we make the short walk back to the buses in silence and pile on. We are, to say the least, exhausted. But filled with something that we all know will never go away. I stow my bag above my seat and slide in next to the window. I saw Jake in line for the comfort station, so I figure he's changing back into his traveling clothes. I look out the window at the thinning crowd.

"Is this seat taken?"

I know before I look up that it's Della.

"No. No, it's not," I say. "It's . . . it's . . . "

"Free?" she smiles.

Yes, that's the word.

Epilogue

Stay here, Will, while I call the city desk," I tell my son. At 13, he's pretty hardheaded like his uncle, John-Two, or as he is known now, the Reverend John Banks, Jr. But on occasion, Will surprises me by actually minding me.

Standing here in the shadow of the Lincoln Memorial, in August 1993, I am reminded of that hot day in August, 1963, when I came to Washington for the famous march. The idea of 200,000 people coming together, peacefully, to protest the injustices of segregation and discrimination never ceases to amaze me.

After the march, we all—Jake, Della, Lo-Tone, and I—knew that we had experienced something wonderful, a once-in-a-lifetime event. I am so glad I had the chance to share it with those special people, and that is why I am here today for the 30th anniversary of the March on Washington for Jobs and Freedom. I'm here with my son and my father, who, at 73, has long since accepted his sons' activism. John-Two is here too. He's still fighting in the trenches every day, from the pulpit to the soup kitchen to the boardroom.

I, too, am still a part of the struggle. I became a journalist and later a columnist for a newspaper in Chicago.

We lost Mama Ev in 1965. She held tough to the end, long enough to witness the passage of the Civil Rights Act of 1964, which made it illegal to bar a person from seeking employment; voting; or using hotels, parks, restaurants, and other public places on the basis of that person's color, race, national origin, religion, or gender. She seemed at peace after that, as though she could finally let go knowing that the door might be open a little wider for John-Two and me. Broken hearted, Grandpa Will died a year after Mama Ev, to the day, for no apparent reason. The doctors said it was "natural causes," but I know he wanted to be with her. He was that way.

Lo-Tone died in 1970, while on patrol with the army in Vietnam. I can talk about it now, but it took years for the hole he blasted in my heart to heal. Before he enlisted in 1968, Lo-Tone managed to become a star pitcher for the varsity baseball team and the first black student to captain a varsity squad at Middlefield High School. I was his catcher, and to tell the truth, I should've been named, at least, the cocaptain. But, hey, one brother through the door at a time, right?

Della went off to college on the East Coast. I stayed closer to home and attended the University of Missouri. After graduation, Della worked in the Peace Corps in Cameroon, and it became harder and harder for us to keep in touch. She met her husband, Donald Goines, there. The two of them were accepted into law school, and the last time I saw her, about five years ago, she was a superior court judge in California.

Before he left for Vietnam, Lo-Tone came by the house. I was home from my first year of college. It had been a tough year, with antiwar demonstrations on one side and a lot of racial tension among white students who didn't think black students should be there.

I was upset with Lo-Tone for enlisting. It was a war, and I didn't want him to die. We knew at least five guys from our neighborhood alone who had gone and not come back.

Lo-Tone could have gone to college; in fact he'd been offered two athletic scholarships from black schools down South. But Lo-Tone said that they'd have drafted him anyway, and he didn't have the connections to get the deferment.

"Look man, I'm not looking for a blessing," he said as we played catch in the backyard, as we had done so many days.

"I'm just worried about you."

Lo-Tone stopped for a minute. He held the ball in his hand. He looked at me.

"Clay," he said. "It's my call to make."

Note: The photograph below and those on the following pages were taken at the March on Washington D.C., August 28, 1963.